DRAKE

MILITARY PROFILES
SERIES EDITOR
Dennis E. Showalter, Ph.D.
Colorado College

*Instructive summaries for general and expert
readers alike, volumes in the Military Profiles
series are essential treatments of significant and
popular military figures drawn from world history,
ancient times through the present.*

DRAKE

For God, Queen, and Plunder

Wade G. Dudley

Potomac Books, Inc.
Washington, D.C.

Published in the United States by Potomac Books, Inc.
All rights reserved. No part of this book may be
reproduced in any manner whatsoever without written
permission from the publisher, except in the case of brief
quotations embodied in critical articles and reviews.

Library of Congress Cataloging-in-Publication Data

Dudley, Wade G.
Drake: for god, queen, and plunder /
Wade G. Dudley —1st ed.
p.   cm.
Includes bibliographical references and index.
ISBN 1-57488-406-9 (acid-free paper)
1. Drake, Francis, Sir, 1540?–1596.   2. Great
Britain—History, Naval—Tudors, 1485–1603—
Bibliography.   3. Great Britian—History—Elizabeth,
1558–1603—Biography.   4. Privateering—History—
16th century.   5. Explorers—Great Britain—
Biography.   6. Admirals—Great Britain—Biography.
I. Title
DA86.22.D7 D83   2003
942.05'5'092—dc21   2002002484

Cover illustration: *The Golden Hind* (Bill Perring):
BPerring@aol.com.

ISBN 1-57488-535-9 (paper)

Printed in the United States of America on acid-free
paper that meets the American National Standards
Institute z39-48 Standard.

Potomac Books, Inc.
22841 Quicksilver Drive
Dulles, Virginia 20166

10 9 8 7 6 5 4 3 2 1

For Dan Kornegay, best friend and best enemy rolled into one—may the dice always fall your way (unless I am on the opposite side of the battlefield!)

and

For Arthur and Dorothy Marske, the best in-laws a person could find.

Contents

Maps

Preface and Acknowledgments

Relatively few people in history have achieved international recognition during their own lifetimes, and even fewer have entered into the realm of myth upon their deaths. Francis Drake, daring to rise above the humble circumstances of his English childhood, accomplished both. What motivated this man? What demons drove him from the green fields of his childhood to chance death again and again on foreign soil and distant seas? This volume offers a three-part answer to those questions: Drake fought for God, for queen, and for plunder.

Born into an era of intense religious strife, Drake embraced the new Protestant faith with a fanaticism all too typical of his time. As fratricide within a splintered Christianity increased in Europe, religious war provided both the opportunity and the moral justification for Drake to exploit his ability as a leader and a warrior.

While serving his God, Drake also served his nation; and at its helm sat one of the greatest of English monarchs, Queen Elizabeth I. Her Protestant kingdom threatened from within by religious dissent and from without by the overwhelming might of Catholic Spain, Elizabeth steered a fine course between survival and destruction. When diplomatic misdirection failed to accomplish her ends, the queen unleashed her valiant naval captains, including Francis Drake, to throttle Spanish trade and fill England's coffers with purloined Catholic silver.

Of course, a goodly portion of that plunder made its way into the pockets of the queen's corsairs. And Drake, it seems, had deep pockets indeed! Born to extremely modest circumstances, wealth (ill-gotten or otherwise) provided his only avenue of social advancement. Unfortunately, England's leading seafarer discovered that money tainted by piracy could never buy the acceptance of his new peers.

The voyage of this book from idea to publication has been far less arduous than any of the voyages completed by Sir Francis Drake—thanks in the main to some very nice people. Frederick J. Heinzen, Jr. (Fritz), convinced me to sign on to the project and served as my agent. Working with Rick Russell, project editor, and the staff at Brassey's has been a true pleasure. The same can be said for the staffs at the Mariners' Museum in Newport News, VA, the National Portrait Gallery in London, and the Prado Museum in Lisbon. Bill Perring of the D'Arcy Collection in Surrey, England, a gifted artist and a nice guy, deserves a special mention for his quick response to the need for cover art. (Copies of the cover art can be obtained from Bill at BPerring@aol.com.) Finally, to my wife, Susan, and my family: Thanks for your love and patience when the creative urge began to strongly resemble stress. As always, those people named and many others deserve much of the credit for what lies between these covers, while any faults of fact or interpretation remain mine alone.

Chronology

1553	Edward VI dies, Mary Tudor becomes queen and attempts to restore England to Catholicism.
1558	Queen Mary dies, Elizabeth I gains the throne and returns England to Protestantism.
1564–1567	Drake sails with John Hawkins' expeditions to the Spanish Caribbean.
1567	Drake captains the *Judith* as part of a disastrous expedition to the Spanish Main led by John Hawkins.
1569–1571	Drake marries Mary Newman on 4 July 1569. He then commands two successful voyages of trade and plunder in the Spanish Caribbean.
1572–1573	Drake raids the Spanish Main, plundering a Spanish mule train of its gold and silver on the Isthmus of Panama.
1575	Drake commands an English fleet in the Irish Expedition of 1575.
1576	Elizabeth I provides money and men to support the rebellious Protestants of the Netherlands against Spain.
1577–1580	Drake circumnavigates the globe, plunders portions of Spain's Pacific empire, and is knighted by Elizabeth I.
1580	King of Portugal dies. Spain conquers Portugal.
1583	Drake's wife, Mary, dies.
1585–1586	Drake marries young Elizabeth Sydenham, daughter of Sir George Sydenham, an extremely prosperous scion of a noble line. He frees English sailors detained by Philip II at Vigo, then conducts raids throughout the West Indies.
1587	Drake's raid on Cádiz delays a Spanish invasion of England.
1588	Defeat of the Spanish Armada.
1589	Drake fails in an attempt to capture Lisbon.
1595–1596	Both Drake and Hawkins die while leading a final expedition against Spanish colonies in the Caribbean.

DRAKE

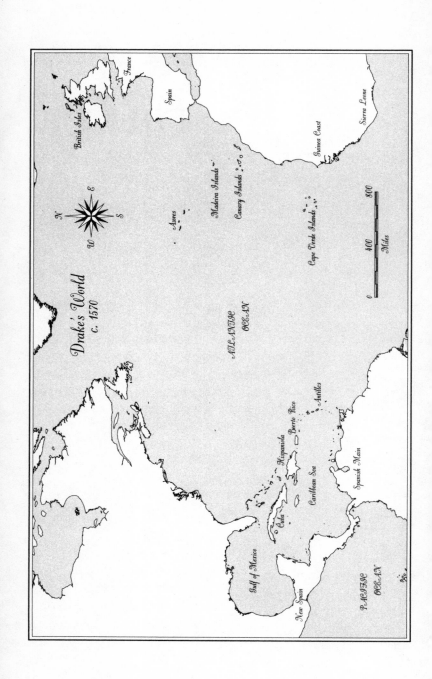

Chapter 1

Prelude

THROUGHOUT MOST of history, the Mediterranean Sea marked the center of the European universe. Propelled by oar and sail, merchant vessels labored along its shores or scooted across its blue expanse, exchanging the wealth of Europe for the food and treasures of Asia and Africa. And as surely as night follows day, war followed those same trade routes. Greek and Persian, Roman and Carthaginian, Christian and Muslim — European states arrayed their warriors against those of Asia and Africa. During the brief periods of international peace, Europeans seemed more than willing to engage in fratricide in the name of hegemony and imperium, or, later, in the name of God.

On the twin bases of trade and war arose the precursors to the modern nation-states of Europe. By the mid-1400s, France, Spain, Portugal, England, Denmark, Sweden, and Hungary occupied prominent places on regional maps. Absolute monarchs controlled those nations, for war demanded a strong hand at the national helm. Across central Europe spread the Holy Roman Empire, a collection of semiautonomous principalities and towns united beneath an elected emperor, and tied to that personage by the vestiges of feudalism and religious tradition. The Italian boot groaned beneath the weight of city-states — Venice, Florence, and Milan at the fore. In Rome sat the pope, Catholic patriarch of Europe's unifying religion as well as secular ruler of the Papal States surrounding Rome.

Blessed by both geography and the Church, the Italian peninsula had long been the crossroads of trade for Europe. Wealth poured into Italian coffers, riches from the Orient mingling with tithes from devout Catholics. Wealth bred luxury, and luxury brought the Renaissance, a rebirth of classical knowledge and an outpouring of creativity at a pace not seen in Europe since long before the collapse of the Western Roman Empire in the fifth century. From the east, along the trade lanes, also flowed ideas — from the humble spaghetti noodle to the printing press and gunpowder. And from the west came other Europeans, eager to seize by force of arms the wealth they could not gain by trade and the art that they could not create for themselves. For sixty years, the Italian boot would suffer the depredations of invading armies.

Throughout these conflicts, trade in the Mediterranean continued — the laws of supply and demand make wartime trade extremely profitable on the micro level (assuming, of course, ship and sailor can survive the attention of both Mars and Neptune). Chief among trade goods were the spices of Asia, craved by wealthy Europeans to flavor often poorly preserved food as well as to lessen the olfactory stress rising from the crowded, unsanitary, and infrequently bathed masses of the region's growing urban centers. Almost as valuable were the silks and cotton clothing of Asia, both superior to the hot, scratchy woolens produced by European looms. But these and other treasures of the Orient filtered first through the hands of Muslim middlemen, and therein lay a problem.

By the mid-1400s, the followers of Mohammed and the children of Christ had been evangelizing via the sword for several centuries (and would continue that deadly proselytism for a while longer). Converts had been relatively few, the dead and the enslaved considerably larger; but the situation had more or less stabilized around the Mediterranean basin. Muslim warriors had ejected Christians from the Holy Lands, and in turn been driven from the Iberian Peninsula by Spanish and Portuguese *conquistadores*. Though conflict continued in the Balkans, the eastward expansion of Christianity and the westward encroachment of Islam had stymied one another. However, the Faithful of Allah had only to look eastward for numerous peoples to convert, while the strongholds of Christianity saw only the cold, fearsome Atlantic waves to their west. And though sea monsters might swallow and regurgitate the occasional Jonah, sailors suspected that the monsters' gag reflex should not be wholly trusted. Worse for the seemingly trapped Europeans, any eastward expansion of Islam guaranteed two things. First, eventually the heathens would have enough warriors to overwhelm the Christians. Second, until that time the Muslim middlemen could bleed the gold and silver from Europe by charging high prices for the treasures of the Orient. Catholic popes and princes found both premises to be unacceptable. Then, in a mere two generations centered near the year 1500, everything changed.

By the 1480s, Portuguese explorers had crept along the coast of Africa in repeated expeditions, eventually reaching the Cape of Good Hope. The gold, ivory, and especially black slaves extorted (sometimes traded) or captured from coastal settlements enriched Portugal and financed additional exploration. In 1497, a fleet led by Vasco da Gama rounded the cape and explored along the eastern coast of Africa. Finding, at last, a willing Muslim navigator, da Gama lunged across the Indian Ocean, arriving in Calicut on the coast of the Indian subcontinent in May 1498. The following year, the survivors of the expedition (two vessels had been lost) returned to Lisbon, holds filled with ginger, cinnamon, and other spices — riches beyond belief. By 1514, Portuguese explorers had reached the Spice Islands of the East Indies, Cathay (China), and Cipango (Japan). They had bypassed the Muslim middleman, and the pulse of European trade rapidly shifted from the harbors of the Mediterranean to the ports of the Atlantic.

From one such port, Cádiz, sailed Christopher Columbus in

1492. The Genoan had developed an intriguing notion that one could sail westward, directly across the barren Atlantic, to reach India. By his calculations, the distance from the Azores to the Orient was a mere three thousand miles and thus within the reach of the small vessels of his day. Columbus harassed the courts of Portugal and Spain for years, seeking state support for a small expedition to verify his calculations (such maritime adventures were hideously expensive and required the support of wealthy investors). Eventually, the king and queen of Spain, fresh from expunging the last of the heathen Moors from Iberia, consented to finance three vessels for Columbus. This investment constituted a major gamble for the war-stressed treasury of Spain, but if Columbus succeeded, that treasury would rapidly fill with the proceeds of trade. And if he failed, there would at least be one less crackpot harassing the Spanish monarchs.

Unfortunately for Columbus (an accomplished seaman who perhaps should have dabbled less in mathematics), his 3,000-mile estimate fell a tad short — by several thousand miles. However, his luck changed with the discovery of islands near a vast and unknown landmass, which saved him from a slow death by thirst or starvation. Columbus insisted that he had found islands near the coast of India, and despite his later voyages failing to discover one ounce of spice, persisted in that belief even on his death bed. The monarchs of Spain were not as stubborn, especially when gold, silver, and jewels looted from the native populations of this New World began to flow into their national coffer. They quickly claimed the mainland and the surrounding islands for their own, then established the colonies and governmental apparatus to ensure that the claim stuck.

Within a mere decade, the two leading nations of Christendom had moved Europe from a localized Mediterranean setting to a world stage. Portugal and Spain stood to garner wealth beyond imagination — if they could avoid conflict along the new trade routes. Desperate to escape a costly war, they turned to Pope Alexander VI to resolve their rivalry. The pope, eager to avoid war among those Christian princes (for money spent on war would never enter the coffers of Rome), issued the *Bull Inter-catera*. This papal writ established a line of demarcation between the Spanish New World and Portugal's African/Asian sphere some hundred leagues west of the Cape Verde Islands, a move that favored Spain (unsurprising, considering that Pope Alexander VI was born in Spain). Unhappy with that result, Portugal entered into direct negotiations with its rival. Those talks resulted in the Treaty of Tordesillas in 1494, and diplomats established a new line of demarcation, drawn from pole to pole, 370 leagues west of the Cape Verdes.

Even then, problems continued. A Portuguese captain, blown far off course, discovered South America in 1500, a fortuitous landfall since a portion of the region (Brazil) fell on Portugal's side of the Tordesillas line. Then, in 1523, the Magellan–del Cano expedition completed the first circumnavigation of the world. In the process, it laid a Spanish claim to nominally Portuguese islands in the East Indies; whereupon the government of Spain suddenly concluded that the Tordesillas line extended completely around the globe. War clouds gathered over the Iberian peninsula, but Spain chose to concentrate upon its ever-more-lucrative New World colonies rather than physically debate Portugal over Asian holdings. Tiny Portugal, sadly overextended by the rapid growth of empire, lacked the population and resource base to challenge its larger neighbor. But the clouds remained until, in 1580, the Spanish war machine pounced upon Portugal, and rapidly reduced it to little more than another province of Spain.

Spanish colonies in the New World supported the mother country's war machine. The oldest of those colonies dotted the Caribbean islands, excellent land and climate for growing one of Europe's most valued commodities — sugar. But sugar was labor intensive, with exhaustion, disease, and the local fauna creating a need for the constant replacement of workers. To silence the pleas of nobles owning these extensive sugar plantations, Spain introduced the *encomienda* system, designating natives of the New World as subjects of Spain and allowing the Spanish nobility to both tax and use the natives as forced labor. Still, the new system of peonage did not meet the needs of sugar planters, primarily because the New World populace, lacking immunity to European diseases, died in droves. Taking a cue from Portugal, planters began to purchase Africans as slave labor, and though hardship still led to short lives, the supply of potential slaves seemed inexhaustible. In fact, a new and extremely profitable triangular trade route emerged. Spanish captains would capture or purchase slaves on the African shores, sell them in Caribbean markets, then return to Spain with trade goods from the New World, parting with those goods to finance the next slaving voyage.

Despite (and to some degree because of) the profitability of slavery, two major headaches rapidly emerged for the Spanish monarchy. First, other Europeans attempted to engage in the slave trade, and Spanish coin paid to Portuguese, French, or English slavers never made its way back into Spain's economy. Royal edicts forbade trade with foreigners, and naval commanders had orders to deny that trade by force wherever feasible. But the New World was a great distance from the court of Spain, and local chicanery often thwarted the mercantilistic intentions of the monarchy. Second, African slaves tended to escape, especially on the mainland. These *negros cimarrones,* as the Spanish named them, often banded together for safety. And if life was harsh and short for those outcasts hiding in the strange jungles of Central America, it was much harsher and much shorter for any Spaniard falling into their hands.

Though lucrative, the sugar industry was only one leg of Spain's New World economy. Between 1519 and 1522, a small band of soldiers under the leadership of Hernán Cortés destroyed the Aztec Empire in Central America. Between 1531 and 1536, Francisco Pizarro repeated this horrific feat against the Inca Empire along the western coast of South America. Ship after ship carried fruits from the rape of these nascent civilizations to Spain —fine-worked gold, silver, and jewels. More important, Spain now controlled the true sources of that wealth, the gold fields and extensive silver mines of the lower Americas. Of course, bullion in the New World presented its own problem. How best could that wealth be transferred to Spain proper?

By the mid-1500s, the Spanish government settled on a method of transport that continued well into the eighteenth century. Each year, after the end of the Atlantic hurricane season (July through November), two treasure fleets would leave the port of Seville for the New World. One fleet, the *Flota,* sailed for Vera Cruz via the Antilles and Santo Domingo. The other, the *Galeones,* sailed from Seville to the South American coast, then cruised northward, loading treasure from colonial ports along the way. One of its most important stops was Nombre de Dios, situated at the narrowest portion of the Isthmus of Panama and terminus for the overland path used by most of the silver mined along the west coast of South America. Rather than risk the unknown waters and storms of Cape Horn or the dangerous currents of the Strait of Magellan, Spanish overlords shipped the bullion refined from the mines of the Andes by sea to Panama, then overland by mule directly to Nombre de Dios; or, for bulkier items, from Panama to the Chagres River, which emptied into the sea near that port. Eventually, the two treasure fleets, deep-laden with the riches of Spain's American colonies, joined at Vera Cruz, then wended their way home through the Florida Straits, hopefully returning to Seville before the worst of the next hurricane season.

As long as storms or accidents did not scatter the fleet, it remained invincible. Its massive galleons, ranging from 400 to 1,000 tons, castles rising at bows and sterns, bristled with ship-killing artillery and large crews of soldiers (to fire the weapons and act as boarding parties) and sailors. Alone, these ships were a match for any vessel afloat, and in the numbers composing the treasure fleet, only a national navy of a comparable size could threaten Spain's New World lifeline. And no such navy existed in Europe. Envy, however, existed in great plenitude. All that other Europeans really needed was a legitimate reason to begin the process of parting Spain from its wealth. What better reason than this, "God wills it!"

On All Hallow's Eve of 1517, as Spain struggled to extend its hold in the New World, a young German monk strode resolutely to the door of Wittenburg Cathedral in the heart of the Holy

Roman Empire. He nailed a sheaf of papers to the door, a document that attacked aspects of the materialism then rampant in the Catholic Church. Martin Luther's *Ninety-five Theses on Indulgences* unleashed a whirlwind of religious controversy upon Europe. The pope sent his best clergy to debate Luther. They lost, and Luther responded with an attack on the essence of Catholicism. Good works, he wrote, were not essential to salvation; rather, salvation proceeded from faith alone and good works were merely a manifestation of true faith. When the pope threatened the wayward monk with excommunication, Luther called upon the princes of Germany for support. Why, he asked, send the fruits of your realms to enrich a Rome that cared nothing for Germans? Why, he pleaded, practice a religion that imprisoned your sons and daughters in monasteries and nunneries? And why, he demanded, do you support a religious regime that keeps you and your people in ignorance by its refusal to allow the printing of the Holy Word in any language other than Latin?

The ousting of Luther from the Catholic Church was followed by war within the Holy Roman Empire, and Catholic solidarity shattered. Of course, Luther's message alone did not account for the internecine conflict. The Knights' War of 1523–24 was a response to the collapse of feudalism. The Peasants' War of 1525 owed as much to the famine engendered by a mini–ice age and to excessive taxation as it did to the interpretation of Luther's message. As for the nobles who flocked to the Lutheran banner, materialism lured at least as many as the gospel called to a new religious experience (in fact, some, such as Maurice of Saxony, would exhibit immense flexibility as war enveloped the empire, changing sides as profit—rather than conscience—dictated).

Nor did the fragmentation of Catholicism stop with Lutheranism; splinter sects appeared left and right as individual interpretation of the gospel led to novel belief systems such as those held by Anabaptists and, later, by Calvinists. Rome, however, labeled all such false believers as heretics, regardless of self-proclaimed denominations, and desired to burn them, drown them, stone them—to eradicate them with or without a recantation of their beliefs. When, in 1529, at the Diet of Speyers, the Holy Roman Emperor ordered all of his subjects to return to the Catholic fold, Lutheran nobles disputed his order. Their letter to the emperor created a new label, which would increasingly be applied to the entirety of religious dissidents — *Protestants,* those who protest. Whether used by contemporaries or historians, that new label is important, for it recognizes that the ongoing religious fratricide was no longer simply a matter of heresy internal to the Catholic Church, nor a problem contained within the boundaries of the Holy Roman Empire. Rather, religious conflict had assumed a decidedly European face and would unite the divergent heretical groups against the Catholic monolith in a conflagration that would spread to the corners of the globe and persist for generations.

Of all the emerging modern nations of Europe, only one embraced Protestantism from the top down and without the trappings of Lutheranism. In fact, England deserted the Church far less in Luther's name than in the name of sex. In 1527, Henry VIII, Sovereign by the Grace of God of England, ordered Thomas Wolsey, Catholic cardinal as well as Henry's chief minister, to secure an annulment of his eighteen-year marriage to Catherine of Aragon. Two reasons lay behind the request. First, Catherine had not gifted Henry with a son, which the king desperately needed if the Tudor dynasty was to continue. In fact, only one of their children, Mary Tudor, would survive to adulthood. Second, and apparently of near equal weight in the king's eyes, he lusted after the lovely Anne Boleyn, one of his queen's ladies-in-waiting. Though Henry had been known to stray from his vows, Anne would have none of that — it would be a crown for her or continued frustration for "Bluff Hal."

Since a frustrated king can be immensely troublesome (if not deadly) to those around him, Wolsey set to with a will. Only the pope could grant an annulment to Catholic princes, but on the surface, Henry had two things in his favor. First, he had married his brother's widow, and, as Leviticus 20:21 warns, such unnatural joinings will be without fruit. Henry had been aware of this verse before the marriage, but the union had been allowed to continue (with a papal dispensation) to ensure smooth relations with Spain. Then, as year followed year without an heir, Henry had increasingly felt the prick of conscience, and the affection apparent as newlyweds had dwindled correspondingly. Second, at the urging of Wolsey, Henry had written (or, possibly, simply signed his name) to a treatise in 1521. The *Assertio Septum Sacramentorum* condemned Martin Luther's attack on the Church, and a grateful Pope Leo X named Henry VIII as Defender of the Faith later that same year (a title still appended to the accolades of the British monarch).

Unfortunately, Leo X had died, and his successor, Pope Clement VII, lived at the sufferance of the Holy Roman Emperor, Charles V, whose armies had actually sacked Rome in 1527. And Charles V happened to be the nephew of Catherine of Aragon — a very powerful nephew controlling Spain, most of the New World, and significant portions of Italy, as well as the Holy Roman Empire. If Catherine remained queen, Charles' dynasty, the Hapsburgs, stood at least a chance of bringing England into the family when the Tudor line died with Henry. Annulment gained little for the Hapsburgs, thus Charles commanded the pope to do nothing.

Henry, frustrated politically, religiously, and sexually, took matters into his own hands. He forced Wolsey into retirement in 1529 (the cardinal would later be executed), assumed the mantle of religious as well as secular leader of England, granted his own annulment, married Ann Boleyn, and — never one to do things by half — seized all Church lands for the Crown. Thus, almost overnight and by royal decree instead of popular choice, England became the first Protestant nation in Europe. The transition (for the moment) was relatively peaceful. Altars and other trappings of the Catholic Church were quietly stored away (in the event the king changed his mind again), new English translations of the Bible and hymnals were printed, and many Catholic priests simply switched their vestments for those of the new Church of England. Though a discontented minority wailed at the change, most English men and women simply continued life as normal, slipping quickly into the new mode of worship.

In fact, the only downside to the switch for Henry was that Anne delivered a bouncing baby girl in 1530 — Elizabeth Tudor — and no sons followed her birth. Thus, in 1536, Henry sent Anne to the block for "treasonable adultery," and married Jane Seymour shortly thereafter. Jane managed to deliver a son, Edward, in 1537, but died only twelve days later. Still, Henry had his heir at last, and the continuation of the Tudor dynasty was assured — if the frail Edward could achieve his majority and sire sons of his own. And, if not, two potential queens, Mary and Elizabeth, waited patiently in the wings.

In 1540, Henry married Anne of Cleves. The marriage, never to be consummated, was part of a plan to draw England and the Lutheran elements of the Holy Roman Empire into closer alignment. Annulled later that year, the union is important because it marked an ever deepening rift between Catholic and Protestant Europe, a rift that a child born that very year would later exploit in the name of his Protestant God, his Protestant queen, and a bit of mostly Catholic plunder.

Chapter 2

Young Man Drake

To be born a commoner in sixteenth-century England was to be born into obscurity. Francis Drake entered this world sometime in 1539 or 1540 — no record of his actual date of birth exists. His father, Edmund Drake, owned a farm near Crowndale in Devon and worked part time as a shearman in the growing English cloth industry. At some point, perhaps a temporary economic recession as England realigned itself within the changing European religious order, he also became an ordained priest in the Church of England. Francis Drake's mother may have been named Anne Myllwaye Drake, and, with some certainty, she birthed eleven younger siblings for her eldest son.[1]

At the time of their first child's birth, the Drake family's financial status was above that of most English commoners. That situation changed while Drake was still a small boy. Henry VIII died in 1547, and Edward VI became the next Protestant king of England. The following year, Drake's father was implicated in the robbery of a (presumed) Catholic, but pardoned by order of the king.[2] In 1549, the issuance of a new Prayer Book in the name of young Edward raised religious rebellion among the staunch supporters of Catholicism in Devon. Many Protestants fled to safe havens. Edmund Drake, undoubtedly marked by the incident of the previous year, abandoned the farm for a naval hulk near Chatham in Kent. There he received a sinecure to minister to the sailors of the port, supporting his growing family in near poverty over the next few years.

Though this unrecorded stage in the life of young Francis is shrouded in the mist of ages, the transition from the rich soil, animals, and steady buildings of the farm to the creaking timbers, tar, and salt of an abandoned ship would have been exciting in the extreme. In an atmosphere of "waste not, want not," owners of ships too decrepit for sea removed the masts and hardware from their vessels, anchored them along sheltered bays and rivers, and rented the space aboard for various purposes. In time of war, prisoners could be crowded into the hulks, often dying amid the squalor of packed humanity. In times of peace, hulks became floating apartments, a pittance of rent charged for the pleasure of rotting planks overhead and the ever-present stench of the bilge.

But it is not hard to imagine a child standing on the high-raised poop and ordering imaginary sailors to set imaginary sails for distant lands. The young Francis might have dreamed of many bold adventures, wooden sword in hand as he defended his ship from those same Catholics who chased his family there. Perhaps his enemies were Spaniards, for he would have heard sailors talking about both the riches ripped from Spain's New World and the cruelty of that Catholic nation to heathen and Protestant alike. He might have imagined himself bringing Spanish jewels for his mother's hair or tossing Spanish crucifixes triumphantly at his father's feet, and seen himself applauded as a hero before God by high-born Englishmen and commoners alike.

Though our childhood dreams may shape us, reality creates the habits of a lifetime. The boy Drake, already dreaming of a glorious life at sea, quickly began to imbibe the lessons of that harsh mistress. Drake was a superb swimmer (an art not common to many sailors of his day) and most likely learned this skill by splashing in the dirty waters surrounding his floating home. Certainly he would have learned to handle a small boat under oars, and perhaps scooted across the waves beneath a much-patched lugsail in search of fish and shellfish to feed his parents' growing family. As he navigated his own tiny craft, he would have watched the larger vessels, the set of their sails and the manner of their sailing. Between direct experience and frequent observation, Drake would have begun to accumulate the knowledge of wind and wave that he would perfect in later life.

Drake may have run errands for sailors crowding the port's teeming wharves. In exchange, they would have given him small coins from distant parts of the world, coins marked with strange images and foreign symbols guaranteed to excite the mind of a boy. More often, they would have paid in words, the elaborate tall tales and superstitions shared by illiterate seamen throughout time. They would have taught him the knots that joined the myriad ropes and cables of every ship afloat. Drake would have begun to mimic their sailors' cant, those thousands of words and phrases specific to ships and the sea. He would have quickly absorbed their oaths, and (as children still do) tried them in his father's presence, testing the boundaries of his new-found knowledge.

"Spare the rod and spoil the child" would not be condemned as child abuse for some centuries, so Edmund Drake may have handled such mischief severely since (as every good Protestant knew) giving vent to oaths risked the immortal soul of young Francis. Undoubtedly, the father pounded the lessons of Protestantism into his son, lessons taken directly from the Great Bible, translated from Latin into the common English tongue in 1539. The boy would have learned that salvation is a matter of absolute faith in God, and that his actions should stem from his faith. He would also have learned to despise the Catholic Church, its grasping, materialistic ways made visible in the fine altars of its cathedrals and the rich vestments of its clergy even as it ignored the poverty and anguish of the common man. If the family's flight from Devon had not already taught young Francis that Catholic and Protestant could not peacefully coexist in England, then he (and all of his nation) learned that lesson well in 1553.

Young King Edward died that year. Only sixteen years old, he left no son to continue the dynasty. His elder half sister, Mary

Tudor, took his place as monarch, and, among much controversy, vowed to return her nation to Catholicism. But with reformation had come economic change as well as a new freedom of belief that would not be surrendered lightly by England's Protestants. Her royal decrees ignored, "Bloody" Mary sent the first of many Protestant martyrs to the flames in 1553. Edmund Drake and his family would have lived the next years under a pall of fear. Perhaps this very fear played a part in the next stage of the life of Francis Drake.

At the age of thirteen, Francis left his home. As with so much of Drake's life, exactly what happened is uncertain; in fact, two versions of his teenage years exist. In *Sir Francis Drake Revived,* set forth by Drake's nephew during the 1590s but first published in 1626,[3] it is said that an impoverished Edmund indentured his eldest son to the owner/captain of a small coasting vessel, probably based in Chatham. Over the next years, Francis honed his skills as a seaman in the confined waters of the English Channel, visiting numerous English ports and, occasionally, those of the mainland. Hard work and constant danger characterized the life of a coaster—daily cargo handling and the ever-present threat of a lee shore. And in the scurrying from port to port, the apprentice seaman would have learned far more than seamanship. He would have absorbed the patois of the Atlantic Basin—mercantile phrases, weights, and measures from the maritime states of France, Spain, and Portugal. Drake would have gained an understanding of the market value of various goods and the diverse coinage exchanged for them. Since low profit margins mandated that repairs to the vessel be performed by the crew, he would have garnered knowledge of the intricacies of shipbuilding and rigging. Most important, as his master aged, Francis Drake would have gained considerable command experience. Drake must have carried himself well, for, as the story goes, a bond of great affection developed between the nameless master and his apprentice. At his death, the shipowner willed the vessel to Drake, who then sold it to finance his first voyage across the Atlantic.[4]

Though the romance of this story is undeniable, recent scholarship has revealed another potential path for young Francis. Records place him, and possibly two of his brothers, as a teenage fosterling in the household of William Hawkins of Plymouth, a prosperous relative of the Drake family. Such fostering was quite common in England, and would have provided unique opportunities for Edmund Drake's sons, as well as a measure of protection from the Catholic purges of Queen Mary. The Hawkins clan owned several small vessels, about fifty tons each, and engaged in trade throughout the eastern Atlantic. When trade failed, they were not above a bit of piracy (at least according to French, Portuguese, and Spanish documents).[5]

The opportunities for Francis Drake as a member of the Hawkins family far exceeded those of indenturement to the master of a small coasting vessel. Seamanship and the skills of a merchant paralleled the first story, but formal schooling probably continued, at least in the rudimentary mathematics required to navigate the open sea, as well as in astronomy and cartography. The fosterlings would have trained in weaponry, from the sword and pike of boarding actions to the bow and musket of distant engagements, as well as in the use of the ship's cannon of that day. Even more significant, Drake would have been exposed to the discussion of national and international politics around the dinner table, a far cry from the price of peas in some tiny coastal village.

Though this second interpretation of Drake's formative years lacks the romance of the older story, it does have a certain resonance of reality to it, especially when coupled with the first factual evidence of Drake walking the deck of a sailing vessel. In 1558, records place him as purser on a vessel commanded by Sir John Hawkins, son of William, on an expedition to the Bay of Biscay. As purser, the young officer's responsibilities would have included victualing the ship, securing beer and wine to supplement its water supply (water, stored in oak casks, would turn to a foul-smelling brown sludge in a matter of weeks), and possibly, obtaining trade goods for the voyage—if this was, indeed, a voyage of trade. More likely than not, it was a case of an English fox amid the French and Spanish henhouse — the rich foreign shipping of the bay. In that case, Drake may well have experienced his first combat at sea and, on the return to England, learned the best manner to dispose of purloined goods and vessels without exciting the royal authorities.

But this return to England held a special excitement for Hawkins and Drake. During their weeks at sea, Queen Mary died of a progressive stomach ailment (diagnosed as stomach cancer, though ground glass or poison should not be ignored as the cause of death for the monarch known as "Bloody" Mary), and Elizabeth Tudor, daughter of Henry VIII and Anne Boleyn, replaced her on the English throne. With Mary died any hope of returning England to the Catholic fold, for Elizabeth I would prove to be a champion of Reformation England. By the end of her reign in 1603, the Church of England would never again face a serious Catholic threat.

Between the coronation of Elizabeth and her death, however, the threat seemed without end. Internally, England's large number of practicing Catholics took Mary Stuart, Queen of the Scots and widow of a Catholic king of France, as their champion. Eventually, after a number of botched assassination attempts against the English monarch, Elizabeth confined and later beheaded Mary. As pressure both legal and physical mounted against English Catholics, they converted, or fled to Catholic nations, or simply died (more so at the hands of their Protestant peers than at the behest of their queen). In time, the internal threat of a Catholic Restoration became insignificant.

At the same time, external threats to Elizabeth's Protestant reign increased. From Rome, the pope dispatched priest after priest to the shores of England and Ireland (controlled by England, and forever verging on rebellion). Watchful soldiers seized most of them, and executions quickly followed, but those who escaped Elizabeth's net spread sedition among her people. The deadliest threat, however, came from Philip II, Catholic sovereign of Spain. Philip's father, Charles V, had ruled the Holy Roman Empire, Spain, and other European territories. In 1556, worn by years of war, he abdicated, splitting his realm between his brother, Frederick I, and his son. Philip inherited the dominion of Spain, the Spanish Netherlands, and the Spanish holdings in the New World.

Philip also inherited a strong distaste for Protestant heresies. A loyal son of Rome, he understood at some level that the free-thinking of Luther encouraged people to consider the very nature of freedom itself. Thus, Protestantism existed as a dire threat to absolute monarchs as well as to traditional Catholicism. Philip, and Spain, became the intolerant bulwark of the Church, and the wealth of the New World flooding into Spanish ports gave that bulwark the sheen of silver and gold.

In Spanish eyes, England constituted the gravest threat to the proper order of the world. In an effort to stanch that threat, Philip had wed Queen Mary in July 1554 (in a diplomatic coup brokered by his father and the English queen). For Philip, the marriage was a matter of state. He had no love for his queen and even less for the English people. Mary, who had hoped for both a loving relationship and a child to seal the Catholic future of England, received neither. Though it is doubtful that he mourned her death in 1558, it is certain that he mourned the coronation of Elizabeth as queen and the return of what had briefly been a part of his realm to Protestantism. But what had worked once could work again; thus Philip avidly pursued the hand of Elizabeth for many years.

Elizabeth had many suitors, and with even more guile than that of legendary Ulysses' wife, she played them one against another until it became visible to all that she would never surrender any portion of her absolute power to a husband. Philip II, in particular, had no chance with the Virgin Queen, though her astute diplomacy hid that fact for many years. She despised Philip's Catholicism as much as she feared the power of his mighty empire. Rather than marry him, she did everything in her power to weaken Spain as she prepared England for the inevitable military confrontation with the Catholic giant. Perhaps the most critical step taken by Elizabeth was the unofficial funneling of funds and "volunteers" into William of Orange's United Provinces after 1576. There, in the Spanish Netherlands, a Protestant rebellion had drained Spanish treasure at a tremendous rate since 1566. But long before 1576, Elizabeth had unleashed her "sea dogs"— men such as Hawkins and Drake — upon Philip's empire.

Queen Mary had forbidden her mariners to infringe upon Spanish trade lanes, notably the lucrative slave trade between the African coast and Spain's American colonies. Elizabeth immediately removed those restrictions. Unofficially, the Hawkins family had visited the Guinea Coast more than once, English port officials turning a blind eye (and a greased palm) to the gold, ivory, and spice filling the holds of their returning ships. But in 1562, John Hawkins planned an official expedition to acquire black slaves to sell in Spanish America. Three or four vessels under his direct command and including Francis Drake among the crew sailed in October of that year. After stops for trade and resupply in the Canary and Cape Verde Islands, the small fleet reached Sierra Leone where Hawkins filled his holds with human cargo. Some slaves he captured, some he may have purchased, and others he certainly stole from Portuguese slavers. When the number of black bodies threatened to exceed available space, he commandeered a Portuguese vessel to handle the overflow. Enriched by both trade and outright piracy, the captain placed his nonliving plunder aboard his smallest vessel and ordered it (with, it appears, Francis Drake aboard) to England. He took the remaining ships to the Caribbean, returning to Plymouth in September 1563 after selling every surviving African to Spaniards eager for new slaves. Each investor in the expedition, including young Drake, amassed immense profits. This did not go unnoticed by the queen, who, despite the cries of piracy most foul from Spain and Portugal, committed to invest in the next expedition by Hawkins.

An eager Hawkins led that expedition from port in October 1564, commanding it from his queen's contribution, the *Jesus of Lubeck*. Though almost three times as large as the remainder of his fleet combined, the 700 ton ship had been afloat for nearly two decades and showed its age. Three vessels, the *Salomon,* the *Tiger,* and the *Swallow,* massing only 220 tons among them, completed the force. Along with the crews, making his first trip to the New World, was Francis Drake. Here, he would learn the measure of a successful cruise.

As with the last cruise, Hawkins obtained slaves as cheaply as possible. Drake probably participated in raids on African villages and quick descents on Portuguese camps and vessels. Holds crammed with human cargo, Hawkins' ships soon sailed for the West Indies. Spanish authorities, warned against trade with the hated Protestants yet needing the cargo on their plantations, joined the English captain in a degree of subterfuge. Shots would be exchanged, Hawkins would land a strong force of seamen, and the local Spanish governor or mayor would either agree to trade "under duress" (at bargain prices, of course) or bribe Hawkins to leave. In this case, Hawkins would strand slaves near the port in a quantity amazingly equal to the price of the bribe. Either way, the English sailed home with Spanish silver while the Spaniards argued to their king that they had been "forced" to accept the slaves.

Drake also learned the value of allies during the voyage. Whenever possible, Hawkins relied on local pilots to guide his ships. His primary local guide was a French Huguenot (one of the Calvinist Protestants of France) who led the expedition to the Huguenot settlement of Fort Caroline on the Río de Mayo. Here, among people who had fled Catholic persecution in their own country, Hawkins refreshed his ships and crews before continuing. This alignment of Protestant with Protestant is worth noting, as Drake would take advantage of it later in his career.

Still, Drake the merchant had to deal with Catholics. And if he never showed the flexibility of Hawkins, who had been known to attend a Mass as readily as a Reformed service, he at least acted with kindness and generosity when feasible. Even when, during and after the 1560s, Protestant services became required aboard English vessels—a sure sign that the battlelines between Protestant and Catholic were assuming increased rigidity—Drake refused to let religion alone interfere with business. Of course, a Catholic who refused to trade was another story.

As soon as Hawkins returned to England, he began to assemble another expedition. All investors, apparently including Francis Drake and certainly including Drake's queen, had realized tremendous profits from the voyage. Still, Spanish and Portuguese ambassadors presented strong indictments of Hawkins' activities to the English court. Shouldering into the privileged slave trade was bad enough, even without the petty piracy engaged in by Hawkins. The queen officially withdrew her support for another slaving expedition, at least until the international situation quieted. She even required Hawkins to post a £500 bond for his next voyage, to be forfeited if any of the vessels entered West Indies waters. This constituted little more than an unofficial wink by Elizabeth, as the loss of the bond would matter little compared with the profits realized by the earlier voyages. Yet it created plausible deniability (that favorite expression of modern statesmen), perhaps the first time Elizabeth used this technique with her much favored piratical mariners. It would not be the last time.

With the queen's quiet nod, Hawkins completed preparations to sail, including bonding the voyage. Then, at the last minute, he placed John Lovell, a kinsman, in charge of the expedition's four small vessels (the total tonnage was less than that of Hawkins' flagship of the previous voyage alone), and remained in England when the fleet sailed in October 1566. Drake apparently served as an officer aboard Lovell's flagship. Certainly both men had something in common—they were hard-core Protestants, strictly enforcing religious discipline during the voyage. The expedition followed the same pattern as previous trips, perhaps with a little less outright piracy and a bit more trading. The sale of slaves in the Indies also met increasing resistance from local Spanish authorities, but subterfuge prevailed when government relations did not, and the populace, desperate for slave labor, circumvented the will of their civil leaders.

Lovell returned to England in 1567. The expedition had been far less profitable than those of previous years, though the size of the ships involved as well as the forfeiture of the royal bond may have been more important in that result than any increased Spanish resistance. Hawkins, displeased with both the profitability of the expedition and Spain's attempt to deny English trade in the Indies, immediately began to plan a major effort for later that year. With the solid backing of his queen, he promised once and for all time to open the West Indies to English slavers.

Drake had returned to sad news — his father had died during his eldest son's absence. But Drake took little time to mourn, though he did see to the welfare of his younger siblings before rejoining Hawkins in Plymouth. Apparently the great captain had not tarred his young kinsman with the same brush as Lovell. Hawkins offered, and Drake accepted, command of the 50 ton *Judith,* one of four ships in the newest expedition owned by the Hawkins family (the others were the *William and John,* 150 tons; the *Swallow,* 180 tons; and the *Angel,* 33 tons). Queen Elizabeth provided two ships, the old *Jesus of Lubeck* and the *Minion* (of comparable size), sealing her personal involvement in the voyage. A tiny pinnace of seven tons completed the powerful merchant fleet.

Adversity seemed to plague the expedition from its beginning. A storm scattered the fleet and sank the pinnace only four days from Plymouth, though the remaining vessels managed to rendezvous in the Canary Islands. Hawkins then sailed for the port of Santa Cruz on the island of Tenerife, his normal stop for watering and purchasing provisions. This time, the local militia met him instead of his usual contacts. Apparently, Spain's patience with England's antics had been exhausted. Only the obvious strength of Hawkins' fleet (and, perhaps his willingness to sack the port if aggravated) convinced the local authorities to avoid bloodshed. As the fleet watchfully repaired storm damage, watered, and gathered supplies, tension without led to tension within. Hawkins and a crewman, Edward Dudley, actually fought with knives. With pride and body injured, Hawkins condemned the man to death, only to pardon him a few days later — a short reprieve, as Dudley died of disease late in the voyage.

Leaving Tenerife at last, Hawkins continued to the Guinea

Coast, adding an unwilling Portuguese vessel and a willing French merchantman to his fleet along the way. Apparently, slave traders avoided the fleet, a strong commentary on Anglo-Portuguese relations, and Hawkins found it necessary to fight for his black gold. Raids on villages, including a temporary alliance in a war between two African kings, eventually netted some six hundred poor souls for his holds. In turn, a few dozen Englishmen died of spear thrusts and poisoned arrows, adding their names to the increasing roll of those dead from disease.

Except for sickness (the *Minion* apparently served as a floating isolation ward), the journey to the Indies was uneventful. After several weeks' sail, the expedition arrived at the tiny port of Margarita in the Antilles, where it was received with open arms; and little wonder, since one of two French fleets operating in the Indies had raided the port some weeks earlier. Hawkins happily replenished his water and provisions in exchange for English trade goods desperately needed by the locals. It would be the last such happiness experienced by the expedition.

Making harbor on the mainland at Borburata, Hawkins met strong resistance from local officials, and the old pattern — seize Spanish citizens or towns for fake ransom in exchange for slaves — did not work as well. More death and violence led to smaller profits. Possibly, the English practice of defacing Catholic churches and shrines contributed as much to the resistance as any fear of a distant Spanish king. Using Borburata as a central anchorage, Hawkins dispatched his fleet in ones and twos to nearby towns. Resistance remained strong; the sale of goods and slaves proceeded slowly. Deciding to relocate the fleet northward to Río de la Hacha, Hawkins dispatched Drake's *Judith* and the *Angel* to reconnoiter — new Spanish forts barred their entrance to the harbor with a brisk cannonade. When Hawkins arrived, negotiations with the local commander failed, so he landed two hundred men and seized the town. Looting and arson accomplished what peaceful talks had failed to gain, and the expedition engaged in several weeks of brisk trade. Hawkins repeated this stratagem successfully at Santa Marta, but the governor at Cartagena refused to trade even when the English captured and looted several warehouses following a bloody engagement.

The constant need for extended negotiations and often violent action had slowed the progress of the expedition. By early August, when Hawkins finally abandoned the pointless effort at Cartagena, the chance of encountering a major Atlantic storm on the homeward voyage increased with each day. Despite the fact that a few dozen slaves and various trade goods remained in the holds of his ships, Hawkins decided to sail for the Yucatan Channel, the Straits of Florida, and England. With his crews much reduced by conflict and disease, he abandoned the Portuguese vessel captured earlier in the voyage and apparently bid farewell to his French merchantman compatriot as well. A few days later, long before it could reach the Atlantic proper, a hurricane shattered the fleet. Every ship suffered damage; the *Jesus of Lubeck* almost sank. The *William and John* appeared to have been lost in the violent weather, though it eventually reached home on its own. When the storm pushed the survivors hundreds of miles into the Gulf of Mexico, a desperate Hawkins took desperate measures to save his men and fortune—he seized the Spanish town of San Juan de Ulúa (the port for the city of Vera Cruz), from which place Spain loaded the wealth garnered from Mexico onto its yearly treasure fleet. In fact, part of the ease with which Hawkins seized the port related to that fleet. The local citizens had mistaken his battered ships for the treasure fleet, which was expected any day.

Hawkins immediately established a battery to command the harbor, a fortunate decision as the Spanish fleet appeared the very next morning. With a new storm threatening, the Spanish admiral and the English captain negotiated a deal that would allow both sides to temporarily use the harbor. For once, however, Spanish duplicity matched that of the English sea dogs. Two days later, with darkness nullifying the advantage of Hawkins' land battery, the Spanish struck with overwhelming force. When a fireship ignited the *Jesus of Lubeck,* Hawkins could do little but transfer to the still-intact *Minion* and try to save as many men as possible. Only one other English vessel, that commanded by Francis Drake, broke free of the Spanish trap. Both vessels, with battle damage now added to that of the previous storm, were in a bad way—crowded with survivors and short of water and provisions. Then the storm, which had been threatening for two days, finally broke. Driven apart by wind and current, each captain had to make a separate way home.

Drake, apparently having briefly anchored at some unknown location to obtain water and supplies, reached Plymouth on 28 December 1567. Hawkins, his crew weakened by hunger and disease despite having abandoned one hundred survivors to the tender mercies of Spain, anchored at the same port three days later. Sick himself, Hawkins dispatched the healthy Drake to London with an initial report of the failure of the expedition for its investors. Those investors were not happy, especially once Hawkins claimed the loss of £25,000. Perhaps the least happy of them all was Elizabeth I, who had not only lost a royal ship and her investment, but had to deal with an international incident of war-provoking proportions. In her search for a scapegoat, it appears that she may have imprisoned Drake for a short time, despite his protestations of innocence at the charge of deliberately abandoning his commander and the *Minion* to their fate. Hawkins would write of the event itself, "So with the *Minion* only and the *Judith*, a small bark of 50 tons, we escaped; which bark the same night forsook us in our great misery."[6]

That line haunted Drake for his entire life. Despite the fact that he and Hawkins would themselves be somewhat reconciled, the tinge of cowardice would remain. Perhaps it was an unfitting end to a long apprenticeship at sea, but from it emerged a mature, angry captain with something to prove—his personal courage—and someone to focus his anger against—Philip II of Spain and his Catholic minions.

Chapter 3

To the Spanish Main
and Beyond

For some months after the fiasco at San Juan de Ulúa, the mists of time dim the life of Francis Drake. We know that he faced accusations of fiscal impropriety — he claimed to have shared the portion of the expedition's treasure aboard the *Judith* among the crew while his detractors claimed that Drake purloined it for himself — to which the young mariner responded that he had lost not only his investment, but many dear friends as well (of the four hundred men who sailed from England, less than one-quarter returned). The queen may have detained or imprisoned him during the investigation of the tragic voyage, but he may just as well have taken time to pursue the one thing missed by most sailors of the era, feminine companionship.

Lending credence to that speculation is the marriage of Francis Drake to Mary Newman on 4 July 1569. Little is known of that lady, though the lack of data itself is revealing. Her family enjoyed neither great wealth nor political connections, hence the lack of surviving information. Thus Francis and Mary probably wedded for love, or, at the least, from lust. Since neither love nor lust tends to fill the stomach, and since the new Mrs. Drake would have possessed little in the way of a dowry, one can wonder how Mr. Drake planned to support a wife and future family. Perhaps he did, indeed, hide away a portion of the treasure from the San Juan de Ulúa expedition. The morals of piracy are not easily abandoned once ashore.

Wedded bliss lasted only a few months before Drake abandoned his wife for his lifelong mistress, the sea. In November 1569, he sailed again for the Guinea Coast and the Spanish Main. Sources vary as to the origins of the expedition, though it is certain that Drake led a force of two small vessels from Africa to the West Indies, possibly with the financing of William Hawkins, the man who had fostered Drake as a child. Once in the Indies, Drake traded English goods, and probably slaves, to the Spaniards. Apparently, he steered away from piracy and direct confrontation with Spanish authorities. This placed the expedition in a decided minority, as the Spanish dominions teemed with French and English pirates that year. Later, Drake would term this a voyage of reconnaissance.

And it is well that he performed his observations before acting in haste, as the situation in the West Indies had changed. Spain had learned, as every nation bordering the great sea would eventually learn, that the Atlantic did not form a moat protecting its distant possessions; rather, it was a highway, easily traveled by friend and foe alike. With piracy increasing, Philip II ordered the creation of an Indies Fleet in 1568. This ancestor of the *Guarda Costa* (which would still be chasing buccaneers and privateers in the Caribbean two hundred years later) was not meant to eliminate piracy from the region—maritime geography made that an impossibility—but to deter raids on shipping and settlements. To enforce this policy of containment, the fleet originally employed galleons and mandatory convoys for merchant vessels. The massive two- and three-decked ships worked well as convoy escorts, as no sane pirate would risk attacking such floating fortresses.

But the Indies Fleet had two weaknesses that the freebooters mercilessly exploited. Its galleons, of broad beam and deep draft, could not enter the shallow waters present near shore, nor did they possess a high turn of speed in any but the most favorable winds. And expense limited the number of ships available; they simply could not be everywhere at once. Raiders switched from large vessels to shallow draft pinnaces of three to twenty-five tons, equipped with oars as well as sails. Working alone or in concert with a larger tender (often a fast, single-decked vessel itself), the pirates cruised the shallow bays, inlets, and rivers of the Spanish Main, looting goods from warehouses and capturing ships before they joined convoys. Meanwhile, other vessels mounted a sea guard, warning when elements of the Indies Fleet finally responded to local cries of duress. Then the pinnaces fled, or were towed by their tender, to safer waters.

In response to the new tactics of the pirates, the Spanish began to build *fragatas*. These single-decked, narrow-beamed, and usually three-masted vessels not only possessed a shallow draft and good turn of speed, they often sported sweeps (oversized oars) for emergency use and carried or towed longboats capable of pursuing fleeing pirates into any waters. Over time, Spanish authorities also increased military garrisons in the larger towns of the region, while constructing blockhouses and artillery batteries at even minor ports. Local militias of varying quality and quantity supported this antipiracy effort.

Drake traded, observed, and planned a return voyage to enrich himself at Catholic expense. Perhaps at the same time he could wipe away the stain of San Juan de Ulúa. His opportunity arose in the following year, 1571. The successful trading expedition of 1569–70 apparently financed the purchase of his own vessel, the *Swan*, a large pinnace of twenty-five tons. Drake captained the craft in his own right, and may have commanded the expedition of three ships that sailed from Plymouth for the Spanish Main, but the Hawkins family or the merchant-adventurers William and George Wynter probably organized the effort, supported by the usual coterie of London investors. Certainly the raiding voyage (trading was not on the agenda) had at least the tacit approval

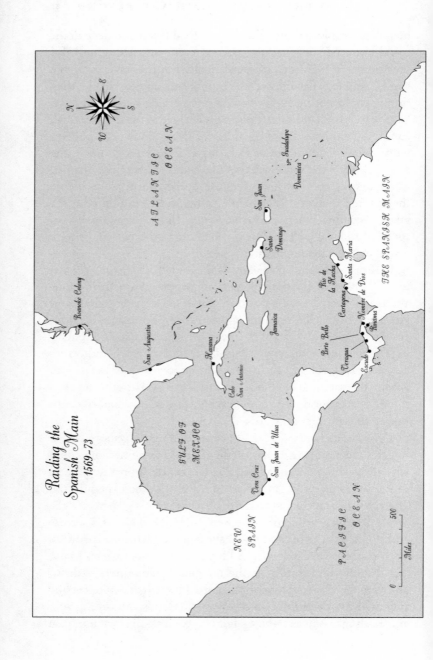

Raiding the
Spanish Main
1569–73

NEW SPAIN

GULF OF MEXICO

Vera Cruz
San Juan de Ulua

ATLANTIC OCEAN

Roanoke Colony

San Augustin

Havana

Cabo
San Antonio

Jamaica

Santo Domingo

San Juan

Dominica

S.ᵗ Guadalupe

Rio de
la Hacha
Santa Maria
Cartagena
Nombre de Dios
Porto Bello
Panama
Teruaqua
Escudo

THE SPANISH MAIN

PACIFIC OCEAN

0   500
Miles

of the queen, something that Drake, hardly a power at the royal court, could not have obtained.

The largest ship of the fleet anchored in protected waters near Cape Cativa on the Isthmus of Panama in late January, perhaps after rendezvousing with other raiders. From it radiated a flock of pinnaces and barges, all aimed at separating Catholics from their wealth. In February, Drake joined with French corsairs to attack along the Chagres River, key communications link with the Spanish settlement of Panama, on the Pacific coast. Rowing upstream in a small barge, they came upon a freshly loaded Spanish merchantman. Seizing the rich prize, they headed for the sea, destroying small craft along the way to inhibit pursuit. After delivering the vessel to his tender, Drake's *Swan* savaged a second merchantman, eventually driving the vessel aground where its survivors abandoned the ship. The Spaniards later returned to their thoroughly looted vessel to discover a note, penned by an unknown hand (possibly that of Drake himself). Its concluding paragraph read, "Done by English who are well disposed, if there be no cause to the contrary. If there be cause, we will be devils rather than men."[1]

Deviltry, however, has a price. The cry for aid by the suffering Spanish colonists at last reached the commander of the Indies Fleet. Its arrival at Cape Cativa forced Drake's raiders to flee, scattering among the shallow bays and creeks of the region, and abandoning three rich prizes as they fled. Unfortunately for the hard-pressed local merchants, the Indies Fleet could not remain in the area, and when it sailed for other troubled spots, Drake emerged from hiding. Again, he raided up the Chagres River, this time looting warehouses of the riches from the Pacific colonies awaiting transshipment to Spain. From his new hideout some forty-five miles east of Nombre de Dios, a secluded inlet that Drake named Port Pheasant (after its amazingly bountiful birds), his vessels ambushed coasters and merchantmen. Riches, and some prisoners, accumulated at Port Pheasant. Then, after one final raid along the Chagres, Drake loaded his three ships to bursting, cached what he could not carry, and sailed for England.

Arriving at Plymouth in July 1571, he cruised near the port for three days, waiting for definitive royal approval before anchoring. To be hanged if captured by the Spanish was part and parcel of piracy, but to be hanged by Elizabeth on a whim or because some international intrigue had gone awry—well, France was just across the Channel; and in France, Drake now had friends.

The good captain need not have worried. Then, as now, success carried a measure of empowerment, especially when it made the wealthy even wealthier. As for Spain, its dreaded *tercios* (infantry regiments) may have spread fear of Philip II across Europe, but England was an island nation, and Spain lacked the navy to convey its fearsome regiments to fair Albion. Besides, Elizabeth knew that Philip still hoped to bring her to the marriage bed, to win the kingship that his many soldiers could not gain for him. Until he realized the foolishness of that hope, she could spend her share of the loot gathered by her sea dogs in relative peace. And Drake had plundered a fortune from the Spanish Main, more than £100,000 in pure profit.

Francis Drake's share made him, for the first time in his life, wealthy. He could have bought a fine home for his wife, become a legitimate merchant, and raised a family in happiness and peace. But "peace" could not bring happiness to Drake—he seemed to thrive on conflict and hardship; a stout heart and a stout body happy only when lifting a Spanish purse, smashing Catholic icons, or braving stormy seas. Nor would "peace" bring him closer to what he truly desired—a peerage, and acceptance by the gentlemen of England as something more than a pirate. Both knighthood and acceptance required greater fame and wealth than Drake had yet amassed; and if harming Catholic Spain could bring him closer to that goal, so much the better. Thus, instead of enjoying peace, Drake purchased another ship, organized his own expedition to the West Indies, and prepared to strike directly at the lifeblood of Spain—the flow of gold and silver from the New World to Cádiz.

In May 1572, Drake led his small squadron of two ships, crowded with seventy-three souls, from Plymouth. Among the crew stood his brothers, John and Joseph. Drake commanded the *Pasha,* seventy tons, while John, second-in-command of the expedition, captained the tried and true *Swan.*[2] In the hold of the *Pasha* rested the planks and fittings to build three pinnaces of ten tons each once in the New World — rather than lose them in transit to Atlantic storms. Atop the dismantled boats, crates of weapons waited to arm the crew for action ashore on the Spanish Main.

Bypassing ports in the Canary Islands, Drake landed on the island of Dominica in the West Indies. There he spent three days watering, provisioning, and resting his men before proceeding to his old hideout at Port Pheasant. Once ashore, he discovered a message, scratched on a sheet of lead by fellow pirate John Garret. Garret warned Drake that former prisoners had compromised the hideout. The Spanish authorities not only knew its location, but had recovered the supplies cached there by Drake the previous year. Undeterred by this unwelcome news, the English captain led his men in constructing a small fort and in assembling the three pinnaces, the *Bear,* the *Lion,* and the *Minion.* Work progressed swiftly, especially when the English corsair James Raunse, who had served with Drake in several of John Hawkins' expeditions, joined the fleet. By late July, work had been completed and the daring scheme of Francis Drake at last revealed itself.

Drake knew that the massed galleons of the Spanish treasure fleets could only be defeated by a national effort; and even then, barring an act of God, the vessels were so strong that success could not be assured. But the gold and silver itself was another matter, particularly the wealth mined in Peru. This had to be shipped by mule across the isthmus from Panama to the otherwise insignificant Caribbean port of Nombre de Dios. In that town, which lacked walls, trained soldiers, and significant batteries of cannon, the treasure would be vulnerable to a lightning raid by a small, daring band of English devils. But timing was everything. Only a brief window of opportunity existed between the arrival of the gold and silver by mule and the appearance of the invincible treasure fleet.

Drake's night assault on Nombre de Dios at the very end of July was disastrous. After successfully destroying the harbor's guns without loss, his sailors quickly seized the royal storehouse, but found it empty (the treasure fleet had sailed some weeks earlier). Then, his men, untrained in land warfare, seem to have panicked in the darkness, perhaps because Drake himself had collapsed from blood loss after taking a musket ball in the leg. The only loot carried with them, as the pinnaces fled to Port Pheasant, was a small merchantman loaded with Spanish wine. For this, the English raiders suffered one dead and several wounded, including their stalwart commander.

Worse, the Spanish had been made aware that a pirate fleet hovered nearby. As word spread, local authorities took action to protect their property from the English predators. When, a few days later, the rapidly recovering Drake raided Cartagena, he found only one coasting vessel in the harbor. When his pinnaces forced it aground, Spanish horsemen appeared to protect it from English looting. Though Drake managed to capture and destroy two small dispatch boats bound for the harbor the next day, gold and silver — the purpose of the expedition — did not find its way into his holds. Then the expedition lost the *Swan*.

Drake's chroniclers, then and now, maintain that, short of crew, he ordered the pinnace to be scuttled in secret because his brother, John, loved the vessel and would not willingly have lost it. A more likely explanation, particularly considering John's later actions, is that the *Swan* sank because of its captain's ineptitude. Drake, rather than smear the family's reputation, may well have covered for his brother, forever clouding the issue. At any rate, John became the captain of the *Pasha*. Shortly thereafter, the expedition suffered another blow when Raunse, obviously displeased with recent setbacks, sailed away.

Additional raiding along the mainland produced little in the way of wealth, though the capture of two ships laden with provisions did prevent starvation (one or both would later be lost to uncharted reefs). With Spanish pressure increasing, Drake abandoned Port Pheasant and built a new camp, Fort Diego, on an island near Cape Cativa in late September or early October. Drake then split his forces between himself and John, but raiding, including a return visit to Cartagena, faced strong resistance and resulted in little gain. Returning to Fort Diego in late November or early December, Drake found that John had died of an arrow through the lung after a rash attempt on a Spanish merchantman. Despondent, but unwilling to return to England with empty hands, Drake resolved to wait at the island until the Spanish treasure fleet returned the following spring.

The men rested and played. Things went well, indeed, until the dreaded *vómito negro* appeared — the yellow fever that would plague Europeans in the Americas for the next three hundred years. In a matter of days, most of the men sickened and many died, including Drake's brother, Joseph. Those who survived would be weakened for weeks, perhaps never fully recovering from the disease. With the expedition reduced to fewer than twoscore survivors, a lesser commander would have burned his excess vessels and returned to Plymouth. Stronger blood flowed in the veins of Francis Drake.

Needing manpower, Drake befriended a local group of *negros cimarrones* through a slave freed in the raid on Nombre de Dios. The old adage that the enemy of my enemy is my friend took on new meaning for Drake and the *cimarrones,* for all hated the Spaniards with equal ferocity. Reinforced by a contingent of the former slaves, Drake decided to take the strongest eighteen of his men and attempt an overland expedition against the mule route to Spanish warehouses at Venta de Cruces on the upper Chagres River. Somewhere during that march, Drake gained his first glimpse of the Pacific Ocean. One can imagine Drake, exhausted and frustrated, swearing a silent oath to sail those waters one day; taking Philip's gold at its very source.

For once on that horrible expedition, fortune seemed to favor the English. They reached the mule trail from Panama just ahead of a caravan ripe with riches. But that day, the goddess of fortune merely teased Drake's men. A *cimarrón* gave away the ambush and the Spanish scurried for the safety of Panama, though the

English did capture a few mules loaded with trade goods. These the weakened Europeans gratefully rode the remainder of the way to Venta de Cruces, dismounting to fight one successful action against Spanish soldiers. At Venta de Cruces, Drake's *cimarrón* allies engaged in an orgy of looting and arson before escorting the exhausted Europeans back to Fort Diego.

The raid, despite its lackluster results, confirmed the vulnerability of the overland route for Drake. Once again running raids on shipping for provisions, Drake ran across a French pirate called Tetu. They decided to combine their forces for one last assault on the overland route. On 29 April 1573, thirty-five sailors and a number of *cimarrones* under the joint leadership of Drake and Tetu ambushed the mule train. After a stiff resistance in which Tetu and other French sailors fell wounded or dead, the Spaniards fled, leaving more gold and silver than the European survivors could carry. As their enemy rallied, Drake's men hid what they could not move, abandoned their wounded, and fled to the coast where their pinnaces awaited them — only to find the pinnaces driven away by frigates of the Indies Fleet.

Drake, the plunder he had sought in his hands at last, refused to despair. He and his men built rafts and floated to a nearby island once the Spanish vessels sailed away. His pinnaces arrived shortly thereafter, loading the grateful men and their stolen riches onboard. Drake then returned to the ambush site, hoping to recover the cached silver and the wounded. Too late — the wounded, including Tetu, had died or been murdered by vengeful Spaniards who had also reclaimed most of the poorly hidden silver. Loading what small amount of plate remained, the survivors of the joint expedition returned to their vessels, divided their plunder, and prepared to return home.

Drake, with the *Pasha* and several captured vessels, arrived at Plymouth on Sunday, 9 August 1573. As the story goes, the citizens heard of his arrival from their church pews, and, family by family, they slipped away to the docks until only the parson remained. There they found that more than half of their friends and loved ones who had sailed with Drake had died, but the remainder would enjoy wealth that few sailors ever found. Above all, those survivors could brag that if they had not tugged the beard of Philip of Spain, then surely they had twisted the tail of the Catholic king's mules. As for Drake, the voyage not only enriched him, it gave him international notoriety — to the list of such vicious Protestant pirates as Hawkins and Wynter, the Spanish authorities now appended Francis Drake.

Over the next three years, the enterprising captain parlayed his ill-gotten gains into a successful and (surprisingly) legitimate merchant business. He purchased or built several vessels, letting them sail for distant ports under dependable officers. Though wealth brought neither the peerage nor the respect Drake craved, it did bring connections at court. Not only did the seemingly reformed pirate lavish gifts upon the powerful members of England's ruling class, including Queen Elizabeth, he actually served for a time as an admiral in Her Majesty's Navy. Furnishing three frigates at his own expense, he commanded a fleet in the Irish Expedition of 1575. If he expected to recover his investment from loot, then he failed to understand the poverty of rebellious Ireland. Drake commanded the fleet at the capture of Rathlin Island, a refuge for Irish dissidents. The action happened ashore, a bloody battle followed by an even bloodier surrender when English troops massacred hundreds of men, women, and children after accepting the rebels' quarter. Drake's part, if any, in the bloodletting is uncertain.

Through it all, Drake remembered a brilliant blue sea that he had barely glimpsed through the jungles of Spanish America. Across that sea sailed the treasure ripped by conquistadors from the heathen lands of Peru and Chile. Part of that treasure could line English coffers if the queen would only listen to Drake's plans to lead an expedition to that peaceful sea. Slowly but surely, Drake gained the support of key government ministers, notably Elizabeth's chancellor, Sir Francis Walsingham. And at last, Elizabeth approved the plan, though in great secrecy. Publicly, she authorized an expedition to sail to the Mediterranean for trade with the Turks. If her captains deviated from that charter and pillaged Catholic ships and settlements, this was something that a queen could not always control.

After a false start in November 1577, the fleet finally sailed from English waters in December. Drake led in the *Pelican,* 100 or more tons in burthen (tonnage carrying capacity).[3] Later he would change the ship's name to the *Golden Hind,* which, as such, would become the most famous ship in the history of England. Following Drake were the *Elizabeth* (80 tons and captained by Drake's vice-admiral, John Wynter), the *Marigold* (30 tons), the *Swan* (another *Swan,* 50 tons), and the *Benedict* (15 tons). On board the vessels sailed a total of between 140 and 170 men and boys, crowded amid the knocked-down pinnaces, shipwrights' tools, spare lumber and cordage, weapons and munitions, and provisions for a long cruise. Despite the official line that the expedition would soon be trading with the Turks, it is doubtful that even the rawest sailor missed the fact that not a single pound of trade goods rested in the fleet's holds.

Plagued by storms, the fleet lost at least one person overboard on the passage to the African coast, but once there, Drake began seizing Portuguese and Spanish ships. Most he looted and released, but he forced a Spanish fisherman to exchange his forty ton smack, renamed the *Christopher,* for the diminutive *Benedict,* and retained a large Portuguese merchantman, the *Santa María* (called the *Mary* by the English), loaded with victuals and wine for the fleet. Drake then raided through the Cape Verde Islands before crossing the Atlantic. Along the way, he had a falling out with Thomas Doughty, a captain of the fleet and a good friend of John Wynter. As calms, then storms plagued the expedition, Drake seemed to focus his anger against Doughty. Blaming him for the expedition's bad luck (superstitious sailors often picked a "Jonah" from their crew when things went wrong) and libeling Doughty as a threat to authority, the admiral executed him as the fleet prepared to winter at Port St. Julian, near the Straits of Magellan. The execution cemented Drake's power, but may have set poorly with his conscience. From this point forward, Drake personally conducted almost every Sunday service, despite having a qualified clergyman along on the voyage. Though Drake certainly used God's words to bend his crew to his will, he may well have been salving his own troubled soul.

On 17 August 1578, with supplies running low, the remaining ships of the fleet (Drake had stripped and abandoned as unseaworthy all but the *Golden Hind,* the *Elizabeth,* and the *Marigold*) sailed for the Straits of Magellan, entering that virtually uncharted body of water four days later. Their larders replenished by easily clubbed penguins, the three ships exited the straits on 6 September, only to be immediately struck by one of the violent storms that still haunt those distant coasts. Fleeing before the storm's fury, the vessels became separated over the next days. The *Marigold* disappeared, broached amid the tremendous waves or smashed against the rocky shores. Wynter, in *Elizabeth,* lost heart and retraced his route through the strait and back to England. Drake, as was his nature, sailed on, for he had a promise to keep to himself, and Catholic treasure beckoned.

At first Drake retraced his steps south, searching for the missing vessels. Then, his crew debilitated by scurvy, he sailed north along the coast of South America. Several times, the fewer than eighty men remaining in his crew skirmished with natives as they gathered green plants, the known remedy for scurvy. Several sailors died, and Drake took two wounds from arrows to the face and head. But the gathered greenery allowed the crew to recover their strength, and on 5 December, Drake struck the Spanish port of Valparaiso, looting the town and capturing a fully laden merchantman, *La Capitana.* The rich haul—enough gold, silver, jewels, and fine trade goods to pay for the entire expedition—did much to inspire Drake's crew and to cement their faith in their captain. It merely whetted Drake's appetite for plunder.

With the addition of *La Capitana,* Drake commanded a fleet again. More important, the accurate charts found aboard the vessel allowed him to plan future actions with some measure of confidence. Continuing his northward voyage, he searched for a place to repair the *Golden Hind* and rest his crew. He finally discovered a sheltered bay on a desolate stretch of the coast, but not

Into the Pacific
1579

N
W   E
S

Guatalco

Panama

Callao
Lima

PACIFIC
OCEAN

Valparaiso

Imperial
Valdivia

ATLANTIC
OCEAN

Port St. Julian

Strait of Magellan
Cape Horn

0   500
Miles

before losing men in a skirmish ashore with the now alerted Spanish. Once anchored, Drake's carpenters assembled the last pinnace stored in the flagship's hold. As his men prepared to careen (the process of beaching and tilting a ship to scrape and repair its bottom) the *Golden Hind,* their captain used the pinnace to search for his missing ships, not knowing it was a fruitless endeavor. Returning, Drake oversaw the careening process, probably working alongside his men as they scraped barnacles and weeds from the hull, repaired the ravages of worms, and caulked gaps between planks. Finally, in mid-January, the three vessels raised anchor and sailed north.

From January through mid-April 1579, Drake terrorized the Pacific coast of Spain's American possessions. Long an unchallenged preserve of Philip, neither towns nor shipping sported adequate defenses against piracy. Even the great treasure ships, which did not sail in convoy, carried few cannon and small crews. Along the way, Drake captured numerous prisoners. Their treatment was, to say the least, uneven. Experienced navigators he impressed into his service. Some prisoners Drake threatened, bullied, and even tortured. To others he gave lavish gifts, then freed them. Even when freed, the Spaniards lived in fear that the Inquisition, that branch of the Catholic Church dedicated to destroying heresy at its roots, would think them contaminated by the Protestants. And the Inquisition tended to torture first, to forgive later (if, indeed, forgiveness came at all). Drake did little to quiet their unease. He proselytized with great fervor, using Foxe's *Book of Martyrs* to illustrate the barbaric treatment of Protestants by Rome. Ashore, his men looted churches and smashed icons. Priests, ashore and afloat, they taunted mercilessly.

Fear, of course, is the most contagious of human emotions. As soon as the unknown pirate appeared, Spanish governors mobilized their territories and sent warships in pursuit. Then former prisoners spread the word that this pirate was *El Draque,* the English dragon who had ravaged ships and towns in the Caribbean. They claimed that his great vessels rode low in the water beneath numerous cannon, and that his decks teemed with numerous

Protestant devils. Such rumors have tremendous power, and despite the urging of Spanish authorities, pursuit slackened as individual captains reckoned a chance at glory against continued existence.

For Drake, perseverance paid tremendous dividends as he searched for the great prize, one of the Spanish treasure ships. At Chule, he arrived too late, capturing an empty vessel, its wealth removed only hours before to a well guarded treasury ashore. At Callao, he captured another, but it had not yet been loaded. Then, on 1 March, Drake found the treasure ship *Cacafuego* at sea. Pretending to be a Spanish merchantman, the English captain edged his vessel closer, then crippled the *Cacafuego*'s sails with a surprise volley of shot followed by a brief boarding action. With its cargo of gold, silver, and jewels, the *Cacafuego* constituted the single most valuable prize captured by any Englishman to that date. The next day, Drake sealed the loyalty of his crew by distributing a portion of the gold and silver plate to each man.

By the end of April, Drake had raided his way along the entire length of Spain's Pacific preserve, leaving chaos in his wake. Near the port of Guatulco, captured prisoners, fresh from Spain, provided the first news of recent events in Europe to the long isolated Englishmen. The crew feasted and celebrated when they learned that all was right with their world. The Protestant Netherlands still resisted their Spanish overlord, French Catholics still murdered French Huguenots, and Elizabeth had neither reconciled nor (God forbid it!) married a Catholic prince. Though singing and dancing at the news of increasing European religious fratricide may seem strange, every man knew that a severe outbreak of peace would have branded the expedition as pirates, to be despised, hunted, and happily executed by all European nations.

Now Drake faced a decision of tremendous importance. His holds heavy with plunder, how would he return to England? Drake weighed three options. First, he could retrace his path through the Straits of Magellan, but that meant sailing along an alerted Spanish coast and contending with the fierce storms encountered earlier in the voyage. Second, he could voyage northward into uncharted waters seeking the fabled Strait of Anian, a rumored passage through the New World's northern landmass that mingled Pacific with Atlantic waters. The discovery of that passage, for at least a short time, would be an English monopoly and, perhaps, a more direct route to future raiding in the Pacific. Finally, the expedition could follow in the steps of Spain's Ferdinand Magellan and circumnavigate the world.

Drake immediately discarded the first option, probably not from any fear of Spanish interference, but rather that it would add nothing to his personal glory. In late April 1579, he sailed in search of the Strait of Anian. Somewhere along the coast of modern Canada, he encountered storms and contrary winds. These forced Drake to abandon his search. Instead, he sought a quiet bay in which to refurbish his vessels, replenish his supplies, and rest his men before attempting the feat that fifty years earlier had cost Magellan four of five ships, all but a score of his crew, and his own life.

Drake found his quiet bay in early June, somewhere near modern San Francisco (the exact location remains a topic of debate).[4] There he befriended the local Native Americans, the Miwocs. Apparently, they treated him and his men, with their strange ways and pale skins, like gods, even inducting Drake into the tribe as an honorary chieftain. For several weeks the English dwelled and proselytized among the Miwocs as the sailors refurbished the *Golden Hind*. Then, around 26 July 1579, Drake, in a solemn ceremony, officially claimed this new land for his queen, leaving an engraved plaque marked with an English shilling to record the fact. Abandoning the pinnace and a Spanish prize, he then crowded some seventy men aboard his remaining ship and began his venture across the Pacific.

The voyage from the New World to the Cape of Good Hope lacked neither hardship, danger, nor profit. Food and water often ran short, and the *Golden Hind* required increased attention after so long a journey. In their search for supplies and sites to careen their ship, the Englishmen sometimes skirmished with both natives and well-armed Portuguese galleons. In the Moluccas,

Drake added quantities of high-value spices to the treasure stored in the hold of his vessel. At one point, the *Golden Hind* came near to total destruction when it grounded on a reef. Only God's intervention, as the crew later explained, saved them when a fortuitous shift in the wind and waves freed the vessel from seemingly certain doom. On 22 July 1580, Drake reached the familiar coast of Sierra Leone, where he briefly rested his men before taking the familiar route to England. Then, on 26 September, a fisherman observed a deep-laden, weather-beaten vessel as it entered Plymouth Sound. Hailed by its captain, one of fifty-seven ragged scarecrows staring with obvious yearning at the shores of home, the fisherman heard him ask, "Is the queen still alive?"[5]

That was the vital question for Francis Drake. If she had died before his return, then the three year journey might well have earned nothing for the bold captain and his crew other than a hangman's noose or a headman's axe. But the queen was indeed alive. And as families in Plymouth celebrated the return of their heroes or mourned the loss of loved ones, Drake soon journeyed to London with a select portion of what would be appraised as more than £25,000,000 in spices and plunder. These, the pick of the treasures, Drake placed at the feet of his queen as he held her spellbound for six hours with the details of the voyage. By the time he retired from her chambers, Drake had become the favorite sea dog of Elizabeth I. Some weeks later, Captain Drake hosted his queen onboard a completely refurbished *Golden Hind*. But at the end of the feast, it was Sir Francis Drake who saw Elizabeth I to shore.

Drake's share of the plunder made him one of the richest men in England. Through the grace of God and queen, Albion's foremost seafarer had accomplished his dream. He had raised himself from the ignominy of a common birth to the hallowed rank of knight and gentleman. Unfortunately, the reverse of every medal ever struck should be inscribed with the words "jealousy and scorn." To be made a noble did not mean acceptance by the gentlemen of England — not for a pirate and a headstrong rogue, especially one with the tar that marked the common sailor ingrained in his palms. Soon, however, the nobility of Protestant England would be forced to call upon common sailors led by rogues such as Sir Francis Drake to preserve their very existence from an angry Catholic monarch.

Chapter 4

The War of the Armada

ENGLAND'S NEWEST knight attacked the task of being a wealthy gentleman with the same effort that he would have given to a Spanish galleon. Drake purchased an apartment in London and often attended his queen and her ministers at court. He also purchased Buckland Abbey in Devon, near the place of his birth, as his primary home. Protestant to the core, Drake enjoyed turning the old Catholic monastery into a gentleman's country estate as much as he loved riding and hunting on the very land from which Catholics had once driven his family.

When the people of Plymouth elected England's newest national hero as Lord Mayor (rather than lose him to London or to his new lands in Devon), Drake invested in numerous properties in the Plymouth area. He also continued to dabble in shipping and trade. Though he appears not to have commanded any of his several vessels in person, the hard-earned knowledge of seafaring and trade lanes that he imparted to his chosen captains meant lucrative returns on Drake's investments. Inevitably, and as befit a man of his martial accomplishments and wealth, Drake was elected to parliament by England's grateful commoners. In fact, the years 1581 through 1584 would have seemed perfect to Sir Francis if not for three things — his peers, his wife, and the vacillations of his queen.

Drake measured people by three criteria — religion, ability, and loyalty. A Protestant who obviously had little use for the trappings of Catholicism, Drake could still, at times, deal kindly with individual Catholics of foreign extraction, though not without a bit of Anglican evangelism tossed into the conversation. The same could not be said for English papists, whom Drake simply would not tolerate at sea or ashore. Similarly, the good captain measured others by what they could accomplish on a day-to-day basis; and the ability to write a sonnet or to parse a Greek verb mattered not at all to a sailor and a warrior. Rather, the man who could quickly reef a sail, splice a stay, or caulk a plank by day, then fearlessly wield a pike or bow and carry his weight in plunder by night excited the admiration of Drake. And why not? For that was exactly what Sir Francis himself did best. Finally, Drake demanded absolute loyalty and desired absolute love from his followers. As a successful captain, both often came naturally; but when circumstances or his actions failed to sway people to his side, he was not above buying loyalty with lavish gifts from his horde of plunder. And, if all else failed, Drake tended to use ploys, threats, and violence to force others to follow where he led.

Unfortunately, Drake's elevation to the ranks of lesser nobility brought him into contact with a new breed of Englishmen. Many of them, born to wealth and luxury, viewed Drake as a vulgar upstart, a creature of the dirty masses who had, literally, stolen his way into their society. Some harbored secret leanings toward the stability offered by the Catholic Church. They feared the freedom encouraged among the masses by Protestant theology, and Drake seemed the perfect example of the dangerous social leveling stemming from those beliefs. As for ability, a gentleman ordered lesser souls to reeve and splice and steer; clean hands, and the ability to sing sonnets or parse Greek verbs, marked a person as above the common herd.

Francis Drake.
Courtesy of the Mariners' Museum, Newport News, Virginia

Portrait of Sir Francis Drake by Jodocus Hondius.
Courtesy of the National Portrait Gallery, London

IOANNES HAWKINS

Aduancement by diligence

Qui Vicit totiens ins Fructis classibus hostes
Ille Vagis HAVKINS Vitam relliquit in Vndis

Sir John Hawkins, son of William Hawkins, the relative who took
Drake into his home as a teenage fosterling. On his first sea voyage,
Drake served as a purser under Sir John. Painting by Simon de Passe
after an unknown artist.
Courtesy of the National Portrait Gallery, London

Queen Elizabeth I, in a portrait attributed to George Gower.
Courtesy of the National Portrait Gallery, London

King Philip II of Spain, artist unknown.
Courtesy of the National Portrait Gallery, London

This modern painting depicts the *Golden Hind* (right, foreground), Drake's command during his raids on the Spanish Main. In the background, to the left, is the *Elizabeth*, captained by John Wynter. Painting by William Perring.

This illustration by Theodore de Bry, done in 1599 and titled "How Francis Drake captured the town of Santo Domingo located on the island of Hispaniola" demonstrates Drake's standard tactic of an attack by land against the town walls combined with a direct naval assault against the town's harbor. In this instance, Drake succeedded.
Courtesy of the Mariners' Museum, Newport News, Virginia

This Spanish painting of Drake's raid on the harbor of Cádiz celebrates the successful defense conducted by Medina Sidonia (center), future commander of the Spanish Armada, and the city fathers. That success, of course, was entirely a matter of Spanish perspective.

Courtesy of the Museo de Prado, Madrid, Spain

Against such closed minds and often closed ranks, Drake's proven abilities mattered little, while his attempts to buy his way into the hearts of his detractors foundered. Some even returned the pirate's expensive gifts, while others did not shy from insulting him to his face. The situation would have been far worse for poor Mary Drake, who lacked even the thin cosmopolitan veneer gained by her husband in his adventures. Her death in early 1583 offered Drake another route to acceptance among his peers. Two years later, he married young Elizabeth Sydenham, the lovely daughter of Sir George Sydenham, an extremely prosperous scion of a noble line. Though this second liaison, as his first, remained childless, at least his new wife moved with ease in the circles of English high society, and perhaps gained her husband some additional level of acceptance therein.

After the death of Mary, Drake spent an increasing amount of time in London. Still a favorite of Elizabeth, he found his presence required at court more and more often as relations with Spain deteriorated. There he again rubbed shoulders with Sir John Hawkins, who, as Treasurer of England since 1577, had rebuilt Elizabeth's navy. Such men as Sir Walter Raleigh, a veteran of the Irish conflict and a strong supporter of English colonization in the New World, undoubtedly spoke with Drake, plumbing his knowledge of those far lands. And Drake, being Drake, constantly pressed Elizabeth for permission to lead another expedition against Spain. She vacillated, tentatively approving, then discarding, one plan after another as already strained relations with Spain threatened to collapse completely.

When the king of Portugal died in 1580, he left some question as to who should occupy his vacant throne. Philip II had resolved the issue by occupying his neighbor and its far-flung outposts. His navy reinforced by that of Portugal, he began to seriously consider a military solution to the problem of English piracy. The Pacific antics of *El Draque* and the public acknowledgment of his piracy by Elizabeth strengthened Philip's resolve even further. Perhaps the last straw for the Spanish monarch was Elizabeth's increasing support to Protestant rebels in the Spanish Netherlands. At first, she had opened her coffers to the rebels; then, as Spain's Duke of Parma squeezed the provinces ever tighter, she had dispatched several thousand volunteers under English officers to aid her fellow Protestants. In response, Philip began to lay the keels for new warships to augment his already large fleet. Despite his protests to English ambassadors that the vessels were to be used to finish the destruction of the Turkish fleet begun at the Battle of Lepanto in 1571, everyone knew that those keels were wooden arrows aimed solely at the shores of England.

Although Elizabeth knew that war could not be long delayed, she hesitated to push Philip over the brink, refusing to accept the fact that he had already decided on a military response. Unlike Drake, Hawkins, and other of her sea dogs, she feared the results of war with Europe's most powerful empire. When a legitimate but penniless Portuguese heir, Dom Antonio, approached her for aid in regaining the throne, she asked her admirals to plan a campaign to capture the Azores, then balked at the drain on her treasury. Several times she allowed plans to raid Spanish possessions to proceed as far as concentrating vessels in ports before withdrawing her approval. Then, in the summer of 1584, she approved a plan by Drake to lead a fleet to the Spice Islands the following year. Thanks to an action by Philip II, this raid would go forward, though its target changed to the West Indies—after a brief stop along the Iberian Peninsula itself.

Crops had failed throughout Spain in 1584, and 1585 looked to be a year of famine for Philip's people. The Spanish king arranged for London merchants to send a fleet loaded with corn to the port of Vigo. When it arrived, Philip's sheriffs seized the ships and corn as partial repayment for past injustices, imprisoning the crews in the local fortress. Only one vessel escaped to carry the news and, as the crew had seized the Spanish bailiff in fleeing, a copy of Philip's writ of seizure to London. This could not be overlooked by Elizabeth, who ordered Drake to sail immediately for Vigo, force the release of her loyal subjects and their property, then punish Spain by pillaging its ships and possessions in the West Indies. Drake, more aware than most that his queen often changed her mind, led his fleet in fleeing English waters as soon as possible, on 14 September 1585, before a recall could reach him.

From the deck of the *Elizabeth Bonaventure,* a 600 ton English navy vessel, Drake commanded the largest private fleet ever to sail from an English port, twenty-one ships and eight pinnaces. Martin Frobisher, another sea dog of growing renown, ranked as his second-in-command (vice-admiral) and the queen's cousin, Francis Knollys, as third-in-command (rear-admiral). Lieutenant-General Christopher Carleill completed the coterie of key officers, commanding the large contingent of soldiers with the fleet. All told, some 2,300 souls crammed the frail vessels.

For Drake, the expedition represented a new plateau of leadership. In the past, he had maintained an authoritarian control of his forces — the absolute monarch of his ships and men as surely as he pictured Elizabeth I as the absolute monarch of England. But Drake may never have realized that a national leader, no matter how popular, spends more time in councils than in actual decision making. He possibly never considered that Elizabeth's frequent changes of mind reflected contrary advice from the headstrong individuals who had reached positions of power within those councils. Sir Francis, a man of sudden insight and authoritative demeanor, learned to hate the traditional councils of war expected by his leading officers. This time, despite some missteps on his part, he would be lucky — there would be relatively little complaint leveled by his officers against the man who had tweaked Philip's nose in the Pacific, then sailed around the world. Most of the officers and men alike seemed to love their admiral, even emulating his habits of dirtying his hands with the work of common sailors and leading from the front in battle.

The expedition reached the mouth of the Vigo River on 27 September, landed at the town of Bayonna, and immediately began negotiations for release of the English merchantmen. Drake led the discussions in person while his men amused themselves, to the detriment of the local Catholic chapel and any readily transportable loot. A little pillage and burning certainly enforced the seriousness of Drake's intent. The Spanish governor agreed to restore the English ships and crews, but acted much too slowly in the admiral's mind. Drake dispatched ships and troops upriver to Vigo itself. Plundering the town hastened the release of the captives and allowed the fleet to reprovision — at Spanish expense. His mission accomplished, Drake remained on Spanish soil through 11 October, an object lesson for Philip II on the reach of growing English naval power. Though the lesson was not lost on the Spanish ruler, the delay cost Drake a chance to capture a Spanish treasure fleet that made port on 7 October.

Drake sailed for the Canary Islands, where an alert garrison's accurate cannons thwarted a raid on the harbor of Palma in early November. Abandoning an invasion of the island of Hierro because it offered little in the way of provisions or loot, Drake headed for the Cape Verde Islands. There he invaded São Tiago, the largest landmass of the group, whose populace offered no resistance. The fleet took or stripped the ships in the island's harbors and replenished its supplies from the copious quantities of foodstuffs available. Here, also, Drake paused to reinforce his authority within the fleet. Whether from insecurity or a legitimate concern at apparent laxity, Drake forced every man to swear an oath of fealty to him. Only Knollys and a few of his officers apparently acting in support of their commander balked. To Knollys, the oath seemed unnecessary, insulting to a gentleman of his stature, and certainly in conflict with the oath he had taken to his cousin, Elizabeth I. Heated arguments raged across several council meetings, but in the end, neither Knollys nor his supporters appeared to have taken the vow. During this time, Drake also sat as judge in several matters, hanging one man for sodomy and a second for mutinous actions (killing an officer).[1] Perhaps these harsh judgments were a warning to Knollys, who, with or without an oath, served faithfully through the remaining voyage.

When Drake finally raised anchor, the fleet carried more from São Tiago than loot and provisions. Only a few days into the Atlantic crossing, men began to fall ill with an unidentified fever. Several hundred died over the next weeks, considerably depleting the force's manpower before it arrived at the island of Dominica in mid-December. A lesser officer may have faltered at this point, but Drake knew that surprise and resolute action counted as much as large battalions. Sir Francis proved his point by capturing Santo Domingo with a land-sea pincer movement on the first day of the new year. For the next month, he dickered with the local governor, burning significant portions of the city to encourage positive results. Hoping for a million ducats in ransom from this former capital of the West Indies, Drake settled for a tiny fraction of that amount. The rude discovery that the shift of power to the Spanish Main had been accompanied by a corresponding shift of wealth left the admiral with only one course of action to consider — what place on the Main should he strike first?

As smoke-shrouded Santo Domingo dropped astern on 1 February, Drake shaped a course for Río de La Hacha. After briefly exchanging shots with its defenses, the fleet continued to Cartagena. Again, Carleill led his soldiers in a night march against the town, while Drake entered the port at first light to attack the local fortress. He need not have bothered to load his guns. The brave Carleill had seized the town with few casualties, and the demoralized garrison fled their fortress at first sight of the powerful English fleet. Repeating the pattern established at Santo Domingo, Drake negotiated for a ransom of the town while his men looted and burned. Proceedings continued for several weeks, Drake's insulting treatment of local religious leaders doing nothing to help the situation. Then, as his men began to fall ill in increasing numbers, probably from malaria, Drake called a council of war. He placed three options before his officers: hold Cartagena as an English outpost until relieved, raid another city, or return to England. In the end, however, Sir Francis alone had to weigh the factors and decide on the final course for the expedition. Barely seven hundred men remained on their feet. What with local prostitutes, individual looting, and sheer boredom, discipline among these men showed signs of rapid deterioration; Drake had been forced to hang several men as examples. Reluctantly, the admiral decided to accept the relatively small ransom finally gathered by the local governor and to begin the voyage home.

That voyage began in mid-April. After watering in Cuba, Drake followed the coast of Florida northward, stopping only to loot and burn the town of San Agustín as he passed. Continuing the northward journey, he briefly anchored at the Roanoke colony, recently established by Sir Richard Grenville and Sir Walter Raleigh. Around one hundred discouraged settlers, their supply ship having failed to arrive, joined Drake's fleet as it continued to England.[2]

The expedition finally raised Plymouth on 28 July 1586. Little more than a third of its officers and crew had survived the raid, and the plunder had been far less than hoped for by its investors. On the other hand, Sir Francis Drake had freed the English sailors imprisoned at Vigo, placing an army on the soil of Spain in the process. He had then cut a swathe through the heart of Spain's Atlantic empire, forcing Philip to divert ships, munitions, and men badly needed for the planned expedition against England to the protection of Spain's colonial holdings. Worse for Philip II, between his conquest of Portugal, his bleeding ulcer in the Netherlands, and the preparation for an invasion of England, his coffers were drained. Not even the wealth of the New World could maintain such a high state of military readiness. Drake's successes caused some European banks to reconsider their loans. Even the pope, pledged to aid his favorite Catholic son against Elizabeth and her Protestant heretics, wavered in his commitment. An English official made the understatement of his age when he wrote, "Sir Francis Drake is a fearful man to the King of Spain."[3] Drake himself cared little that a Catholic monarch wanted his head on a pike—this was nothing new for an old pirate. Besides, even as he set foot ashore after his raid, his attention already appeared focused on the next expedition.

Drake, his queen, and all Europe well knew that Philip II had planned and was busily implementing a Great Endeavor. For most of the decade, ever since the conquest of Portugal, the Spanish sovereign's orders for cannon, lumber, masts, ship fittings, and now cooper's stores (barrel staves and banding) and provisions, had stretched across the continent. Numerous hulls, great and small, rode at anchor or lay at dockside in the harbors of the Iberian Peninsula awaiting the finishing touches—canvas, guns, provisions, and crews—before sailing. Europeans also knew that as soon as Philip completed his preparations, perhaps in the summer of 1587, Admiral Don Alvaro de Bazán, Marquis de Santa Cruz, would lead this Armada to the English Channel. There he would brush aside or destroy the vessels of Elizabeth I, embark the army of Alexander Farnese, Duke of Parma, from the ports of Flanders, and restore Albion to the Catholic fold.

Drake asked for permission to lead an expedition against Spanish ports. His queen, hoping to avoid outright war, refused. Drake pleaded for a command to hurt the Spaniards, and Elizabeth dispatched him to the Netherlands as her envoy. The minute he returned to court, he again begged for permission to strike before the Spanish Armada completed readying for sea. Still, she dithered. Then, in March 1587, under pressure from most of her key advisers, especially Chancellor Walsingham, Elizabeth relented. She ordered Sir Francis to harass the Armada within its ports, interdict coastal shipping, and, if feasible, take Spanish treasure ships. Drake, within days of receiving his orders and without taking the time to complete provisioning, led his fleet clear of Plymouth harbor. His last message to Walsingham read: "The wind commands me away. Our ship's under sail. God grant we may live in His fear as the enemy may have cause to say that God doth fight for Her Majesty as well abroad as at home. . . . Haste!" [4]

It was well that Drake, more than familiar with the changing moods of Elizabeth, made such haste. Barely had the sails of the expedition dipped below the horizon when a royal messenger, bearing much more limited orders, galloped into Plymouth. A fast-sailing pinnace with the letter aboard hastened after Drake—and failed to find him. Perhaps stormy weather interfered with the search, or possibly, the pinnace stopped to capture a prize; but an even more likely reason that Drake escaped recall concerns the pinnace's captain. He was a younger son of the Hawkins family, a clan whose hatred for Spain rivaled that of Drake; and any Hawkins would have seen little reason to stop an act that would precipitate the long desired war against the bastion of Catholicism.

From the deck of the *Elizabeth Bonaventure,* Sir Francis commanded a fleet of sixteen ships and seven pinnaces carrying almost three thousand men. William Borough, a navigator of some renown though little experienced in raiding, served as his vice-admiral on the *Golden Lion.* As usual, various investors, including the queen, had funded the expedition. Then, within a day or so of the fleet leaving port, it appeared that they would lose their investment. For four days, a tremendous storm pounded and scattered the expedition. Drake, upon arriving at the agreed upon rendezvous near Lisbon, could not have known if the bulk of his forces had survived. Undoubtedly he prayed for heavenly aid, and no doubt thanked his Protestant God profusely when all but one pinnace finally joined him. Soon, his ships had snapped up several Portuguese prizes; one he kept to replace the lost pinnace, exchanging its crew for five English sailors. But the true benefit resulting from the captures was intelligence: in Cádiz could be found a massive concentration of shipping, including galleons of the Armada, supply vessels, and local merchantmen. More important, word of Drake's fleet had not yet reached the garrison commander.

Bowing to a despised tradition, Drake called his captains together for a council of war. Borough suggested caution — see and test the defenses of Cádiz before planning an attack. Drake listened, but the voice to which he listened longest came from within himself rather than his captains. Years of raiding had taught Sir Francis the value of sudden assault, especially when outnumbered by the enemy. When, at the end of the meeting, Drake ordered the fleet to set sail for Cádiz, Borough requested specific orders. The reply, couched in the simplest of terms, probably left the vice-admiral shaking his head. His admiral simply said, "Follow me."

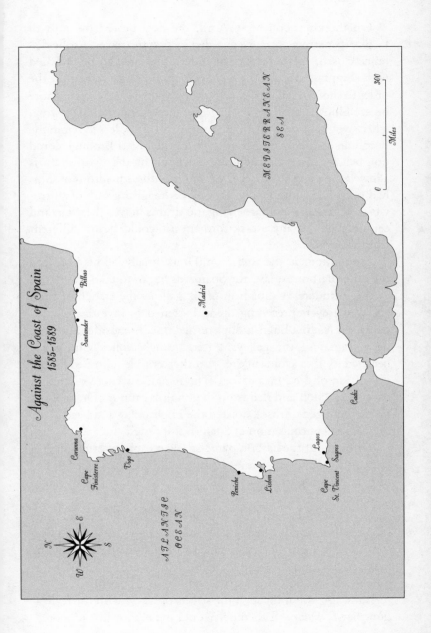

Against the Coast of Spain
1585–1589

ATLANTIC OCEAN

MEDITERRANEAN SEA

Cape Finisterre
Coruña
Vigo
Peniche
Lisbon
Lagos
Cape St. Vincent
Sagres
Cadiz
Santander
Bilbao
Madrid

0   300
Miles

N
E
W
S

On the afternoon of 19 April, the fleet neared the port of Cádiz, its narrow entrance guarded by two fortresses. As the distance closed, the outer harbor indeed appeared to be crowded with shipping. Aboard the *Golden Lion,* Borough waited for the order to shorten sail. Imagine his horror when Drake, an onshore breeze filling the sails of his flagship, showed no sign of slowing. There would be no council, no waiting for stragglers to rejoin the fleet, and assuredly no parley with the enemy. If Borough could not believe his eyes, then the garrisons of the Spanish forts allowed their eyes to be deceived. For months, squadrons of ships had been filing into Cádiz. Drake's bedraggled group of storm-wracked vessels — no flags flying, no drums bravely beating, and certainly not in any attack formation — could be no different from the others.

Around four in the afternoon, Drake finally led his fleet into the outer harbor. At last, the Spaniards began to take an interest in the intruders. A squadron of six galleys, the stench of their enslaved rowers preceding them, hastened to investigate. Suddenly, the leading English ships turned their broadsides upon the light frames of the galleys. After a single volley, one galley beached itself to avoid sinking. Another, crippled, limped for the protection of the inner harbor. The remainder chose discretion over destruction and fled from the English cannon. Drake, with no further need of ruses, hoisted the English flag and headed for the nearest concentration of Spanish shipping.

Throughout the harbor, panic-stricken captains attempted to escape their attackers. Some twenty small vessels managed to flee upriver to the port of Santa María. A few ships, mainly those equipped with sweeps, hastened into the inner harbor. Most simply ran afoul of each other or grounded as their crews tumbled into boats and rowed quickly ashore. Then one ship, a 1,000 ton monster from Genoa, decided to fight its way clear of the harbor. Surrounded by the smaller English warships, however, it quickly succumbed to massed broadsides and boarding.

Panic also swept through the streets of Cádiz with the realization that *El Draque* had come. Would the man who had looted, raped, murdered, and burned in numerous Spanish towns in the Indies spare their city? Fearing the worst, a mob sought sanctuary in the citadel, only to discover that the garrison commander had barred its gates. More than two dozen women and children died in the stampede for safety.

By dusk, Drake had secured the outer harbor. Then the real work began as his men went from trapped ship to trapped ship, looting each in turn before consigning it to the flames. Soon, six thousand Spanish reinforcements, commanded by the Duke of Medina Sidonia, began to arrive in Cádiz. But cavalry and infantry could only forestall any English attempt to gain a foothold ashore; they could not salvage the situation afloat. And there the scene resembled the Christian vision of Hell: a lurid red glare from burning vessels reflecting from the clouds of smoke smothering the harbor, pierced by the screams of the dying and the occasional roar of the great guns.

Amid the inferno, Borough left the *Golden Lion* and climbed to the deck of the *Elizabeth Bonaventure* shortly before dawn. Drake, so clearly in his element, quite possibly never really heard his vice-admiral's counsel that enough had been accomplished, and that, since a steady wind now blew offshore, the fleet should leave before the Spaniards managed to organize and trap them within the harbor. Clearly, as Borough returned to his ship, he expected to see a signal from Drake soon ordering the fleet clear of Cádiz. Yet when the first light of a new day penetrated the smoke, he beheld a flotilla of English boats forcing the inner harbor, supported by a single warship. Borough, obviously less than pleased with his admiral, again visited the flagship, only to discover that Drake had led the assault on the inner harbor in person. Borough entered the inner harbor itself, but could not find his commander amid the confusion of boarding and burning. Stopping at the supporting warship, he found it under assault by several galleys, and ordered it back to the outer harbor. Finally, he returned to the *Elizabeth Bonaventure* shortly after Drake, and made the mistake of criticizing Sir Francis to his face. Heated words followed, Drake later insisting that Borough had trembled from fear of the Spaniards, to which charge the vice-admiral replied that his fear had been for the expedition of which Drake had obviously lost control.

On his return to his ship, Borough discovered that it was under fire from newly emplaced artillery. With one man wounded and damage below the waterline, he withdrew to a position some five miles closer to the harbor mouth. Drake, noting that the position would cover the withdrawal of the remainder of the fleet, reinforced the *Golden Lion*. By noon, the destruction within the inner harbor had been completed, and Drake ordered the fleet to proceed to the Atlantic, but within minutes the wind had died. Becalmed within an enemy harbor, Drake formed his ships for defense against the ten galleys remaining in the port. Though the galleys managed to isolate and capture one vessel — the small Portuguese ship — and its five-man crew, they could not dent the main English formation. With the coming of darkness, the Spanish sent fireships against the expedition, accomplishing little except burning the few vessels overlooked by the English. Around two in the morning of 20 April, the wind returned, and Sir Francis led his tired crews to the relative safety of the open sea.

By Drake's reckoning, he had sunk two galleys and thirty-three other vessels ranging in size up to 1,200 tons. Four vessels, once laden with supplies for the Armada, now sailed as floating storehouses for his fleet. For that result, the expedition had traded one small ship captured, its five-man crew dead, and one man (aboard the *Golden Lion*) wounded. Spanish sources reported fewer ships lost — and even tried to claim a defensive victory because they prevented the burning of Cádiz. But *El Draque* had only just begun to wreak havoc on the Iberian coast.

Between 20 April and 22 May, Sir Francis scourged Spanish shipping bound from the Mediterranean Sea to northern Spain. First, he seized the port of Sagres on Cape St. Vincent for a base of operations, leading the assault on its fortifications in person. There the expedition procured vegetables to treat the scurvy now present in the fleet. He also dealt with Borough, who had sent a missive to Drake challenging him for leadership of the fleet.

Stripping the vice-admiral of his rank, Sir Francis ordered him confined to his cabin aboard the *Golden Lion* to await trial for cowardice in England.

Operating from Sagres, the English captured, stripped, and scuttled vessel after vessel. Even the local fishing fleets met the torch. Not content with the destruction of the portion of the Armada in Cádiz, Drake blockaded Lisbon for two days, attempting to entice Santa Cruz to sally forth with his squadrons anchored therein. But the commander of the Armada had few ships ready to fight — most were awaiting the masts, sails, and cables carried in the merchant vessels that Drake had been busily sinking, or that chose to rot in port rather than risk a meeting with the English devils. By late May, Drake wrote that "it hath pleased God that we have taken forts, ships, barks, carvels, and divers other vessels more than a hundred, most laden, some with oars for galleys, planks and timber for ships and pinnaces, hoops and pipe-staves for cask, with many other provisions for this great army."[5]

By the third week of May, scurvy and fever had decimated Drake's crews. The ships themselves needed careening and, in some cases, major repairs. On 22 May, the admiral divided his fleet, dispatching all but the nine most seaworthy and the *Golden Lion* (with Borough still in his cabin) to England. Then Drake and his reduced squadron disappeared into the Atlantic. Philip II quickly divined the next target, the Spanish treasure fleet, and dispatched every available ship to find Drake. But the Atlantic is a very large body of water. Drake missed the treasure fleet, and the Spanish naval forces failed to find Drake. By the time Philip's worn ships returned to harbor, it would be too late for an invasion of England in 1587 — Drake and his men had purchased their country another year in which to prepare for the Catholic onslaught.

Meanwhile, Drake searched in vain for his enemy. Frustration constantly increasing, he was incensed when the *Golden Lion* slipped away for home one dark night. Trying Borough in absentia, the admiral condemned the mutinous coward to death. But an accidental meeting at sea greatly improved Drake's humor. On 9 June, he sighted the *San Felipe,* a forty gun galleon transporting spices and silks, among other treasures, from the East Indies. The next morning, Sir Francis approached with three of his ships, pretending to be fellow Spaniards. Though the captain of the galleon discovered the ruse, it was too late. Ranging close alongside, the small English ships maintained a hot fire on the larger enemy, whose guns could not depress far enough to hit its opponents. Eventually, their officers dead or wounded, the Spanish crew struck. The delighted English discovered that the treasure ship had also been loaded with the cargo of a leaking companion — an immense horde of plunder that few among the crew had ever beheld.

On 26 June 1587, the fleet and its wondrous prize anchored safely in Plymouth. Ecstatic investors, including Elizabeth, soon welcomed Drake to London. And for once the citizens of Plymouth did not have a staggering butcher's bill to mourn. But Drake had done a far greater service to England than most of its hardy souls realized. Sir Francis himself jested that he had "singed the beard" of the king of Spain. There is some truth in that — the smoke of Cádiz (and of Philip's singed beard) wafted across Catholic Christendom. Its cloud marred the image of success that Philip had carefully cultivated among other heads of state. Its stench strained the relationship of the Spanish monarch and his bankers. Even the pope, far removed from the Atlantic at his palace in Rome, speculated that if one Englishman — this Drake — could do so much damage, then any attempted invasion of England seemed doomed before it began. At Cádiz, Drake began the shattering of Catholic solidarity, and helped guarantee the survival of Protestantism.

On the other hand, the raid on Cádiz infuriated Philip. Not only had Drake burned his ships, he had fouled the very soil of Spain with his presence. The king pushed Santa Cruz to repair the damage, gather new ships, and avenge the English insults as soon as feasible. His admiral began that process, but died in February 1588. Philip selected Don Alonso de Guzmán el Bueno,

Duke of Medina Sidonia and Captain General of Andalusia, the man who had supposedly saved Cádiz from Drake, to prepare and lead the new fleet. With tremendous administrative talent, the expedition's new commander had his force ready for sea by May. In a final report, he tallied every aspect of the fleet, from ship names and tonnages to the tons of provisions and even the number of priests accompanying the expedition. Medina Sidonia referred to his command as *La felicissima armada*—the blessed fleet. Other Spaniards considered its power, then applied the name that has resounded through history, *La Invencible Armada*. Unfortunately for Philip II, the great Spanish fleet would be neither blessed nor invincible.

The Armada sailed in May, but storms and adverse winds prevented it reaching the Lizard (the southernmost point of England) before 19 July. Its strength stood at 125 ships, all told (four galleys, unsuited to Atlantic waves, and one ship had already fled to various ports of refuge). Fewer than three dozen of these had been designed as warships. The remainder consisted of hastily converted merchantmen, transport vessels, and almost two dozen pinnaces and other small scouting craft.[6]

A number of weaknesses, aside from storm damage, already plagued the expedition. Its squadron groupings reflected the diverse origins of the vessels (for example, the Andalusian Squadron and the Levant Squadron) rather than tactical entities. Much of its artillery lacked naval gun carriages and could not be hauled inboard for reloading, thus slowing the rate of fire. For this reason (as well as tradition), Medina Sidonia planned to force boarding actions, using the Spanish soldiers packing his ships to overwhelm the smaller English crews. Unfortunately, those soldiers seemed inclined to squabble with the sailors manning their own vessels when no English ships were in the offing. Finally, coopers had been forced to use green wood for the barrels holding water and provisions for the fleet (green wood supports the rapid growth of various bacteria, thus fouling the contents that much more quickly). The destruction visited by Drake upon Spanish stores the previous year led directly to the dysentery prevalent within the Armada in 1588; by the time of its arrival in English waters, hundreds of its thirty thousand sailors and soldiers suffered from dysentery, scurvy, or fever.

Elizabeth and her sea dogs had not been idle since Drake's return. Numerous small expeditions plagued Spanish communications along the Iberian coast. Organized by private investors, Sir Francis probably among them, these forces did little damage but did serve as an early warning system. The queen also selected a fleet admiral, Lord Charles Howard of Effingham, to lead England's massed ships against the Armada. That begs the question: why not Drake? Certainly Drake had earned the reputation of an effective captain-general at Cádiz. Possibly the conflict with Borough, whom the queen found innocent of wrongdoing (after considering his political connections and reviewing the false testimony of his crew), led Elizabeth to question Drake's ability to handle several headstrong squadron commanders. Most likely, Elizabeth knew that Howard would use his head, while she suspected that Drake would follow his heart—still and always the heart of a pirate. So Howard became lord admiral with Drake as his vice-admiral—and, amazingly, they worked together in respectful harmony.

Howard rejected the suggestion that Drake lead another major expedition to the Iberian coast, and decided to meet the Armada in or near English waters. Over the course of the coming conflict, some 197 vessels and almost 16,000 men would serve under Howard's flag.[7] A substantial portion of that force, however, would never see action. Perhaps 140 ships would actually engage the Armada; of those, fewer than thirty had been built as warships. Hastily armed merchantmen, their crews stiffened with soldiers, formed the remainder.

In direct contrast to Medina Sidonia, Howard possessed several important advantages. Most of his warships were nimble, race-built galleons, narrow of beam with a gun-deck above the hold, and all sported naval carriages for their larger guns. Though Howard's converted merchantmen (and some of his galleons) were smaller than the ships of the Armada, none transported extra supplies and troops—all served exclusively as gun platforms. Most important, the majority of his officers and men had experience of war at sea (thanks to years of piracy) and knew the English Channel like the back of their hand. Also, the English captains operated close to their home ports, readily available havens and logistical centers. With these advantages, Howard would seek a gunnery duel, racing into range, unleashing broadsides, and, if necessary, resupplying powder and shot from local ports. Finally, every man in the fleet, from Howard and Drake on down, fought for God and queen; and if the Armada managed to land a Catholic army in England, both Protestant God and Protestant queen would be at grave risk.

In May and June, the same Atlantic weather that plagued the Spanish forced three English sorties to return to Plymouth. When, on 19 July, the *Golden Hind* (not Drake's former ship, but one of its many namesakes) rushed into Plymouth with the news that the Armada had been sighted off the Lizard, legend claims that Francis Drake was enjoying a game of bowls on Plymouth Hoe. Apprised of the situation, he smiled and said that there was time both to finish the game and to beat the Spaniards. In truth, there was time—the fleet lay wind-bound; the wind blowing directly into the harbor prevented its sailing. Only by kedging and warping (dropping an anchor in the direction of desired movement, then using the capstan to pull the vessel to the anchor's location) could the ships achieve the sea. It would take almost thirty-six hours of back-breaking labor before the bulk of the English fleet joined Howard's *Ark* (800 tons) and Drake's *Revenge* (500 tons) at sea. During that time, Medina Sidonia missed his golden opportunity to blockade the bulk of the English fleet in Plymouth or to destroy it piecemeal. Then, early on July 21, the wind shifted to the English advantage, and Howard, dividing his force between himself and Drake, attacked.

The Spaniards, in their standard crescent formation, heaviest ships in the center and backed by a small reserve, attempted to isolate individual English ships for boarding, but Howard and Drake fought in two lines, each ship turning to present its broadside then making way for the next. Though damage mounted, neither side managed to disable a single one of its opponent's ships. But after the fleets had disengaged, disaster struck the Spanish fleet when powder ignited aboard the *San Salvador,* flagship of the Guipúzcoa Squadron. While that vessel burned, two other ships, perhaps distracted by the explosion, collided. The flagship of the Andalusian Squadron, *Nuestra Señora del Rosario,* suffered damage to its masts and rigging during the collision. The Spanish admiral eventually abandoned the burning hulk, expecting it to sink, as well as the damaged *Rosario,* hoping that its captain could make his way to safety or rejoin the Armada later that night.

Meanwhile, Howard called a council aboard the flagship. To Drake he gave the privilege of leading the pursuit as the Armada lumbered up the Channel, while showing a lantern at his stern for the fleet to follow. As darkness fell, Drake proceeded to validate the queen's selection of Howard as lord admiral. He did not pursue the Armada, he did not show a lantern, but he did follow the path of the damaged *Rosario,* accepting its surrender the following morning. Confronted by Howard, Drake gave the excuse that he had sailed away to investigate a strange sail, only to stumble upon the disabled Spanish ship at dawn. In truth, Drake had just been himself—a pirate—no matter the cost to others.

Howard seems to have accepted Drake's argument, even if others did not (especially when they heard the rumor that *Rosario,* one of the Armada's pay ships, had carried an estimated 50,000 ducats onboard, though Drake reported only half of that amount to Howard). Certainly the capture did not stop Drake from participating in the running battle that raged through 25 July, though it is possible that he had to briefly retire from the action to repair severe damage to his mast, yards, and rigging. For the next two days, there was little or no action, as Howard secured additional powder and shot for his overworked guns, then shadowed the Armada at a distance as it made for the planned union with the Duke of Parma's army. Both forces arrived off Calais on 27 July, the Armada anchoring in the only

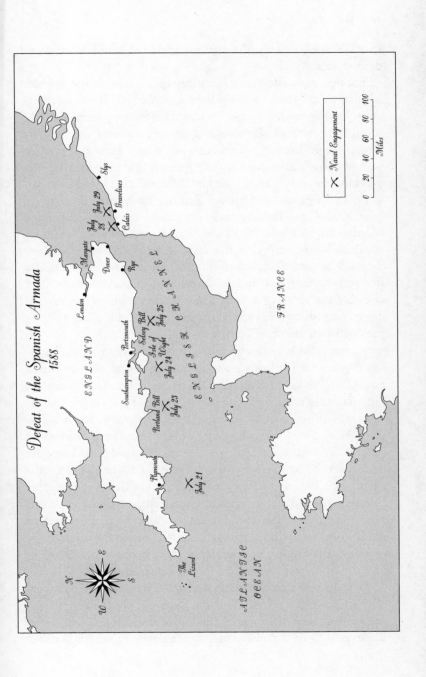

Defeat of the Spanish Armada
1588

location along that shoaling shore capable of handling its deep-draft vessels.

For two days, the fleets, at an impasse, rested, as the Spanish admiral waited for word from Parma. In the early morning hours of 29 July, Spanish lookouts spotted two burning ships floating toward the Armada. Howard had decided to force the issue by sending eight fireships, their cannons loaded and extra powder packed aboard, drifting into the Spanish fleet. Medina Sidonia expected the attack, and blessed by the premature ignition of two of the fireships, ordered his captains to simply move aside while boats pushed the flaming hulls away from the fleet. The attack failed to burn a single ship of the Armada, but the attack still succeeded. Spanish captain after captain panicked and cut their cables. The great fleet drifted from the anchorage, disordered by tide and wind. Ships collided, the galleass (a large, fast war galley) *San Lorenzo* drifting ashore while Spain's admiral fumed. At dawn, English crews swarmed the galleass, stripping it — a fitting prelude to the Battle of Gravelines waged that day.

Howard and his captains fell upon the disorganized and confused Armada, Drake's squadron leading the assault. For nine hours, English cannon roared with telling effect. Before Medina Sidonia could reconstruct some semblance of a defensive formation, two of his powerful ships had been forced to beach themselves (easy prey for the English) while a third sank, riddled by accurate Protestant fire. As darkness fell, Howard pulled his fleet back from the battered Armada, leaving Medina Sidonia a difficult choice. He had to either make for port at Calais to repair his battered fleet, or flee northward, then circle Ireland to return home. In the end, however, he had no choice at all when a definitely Protestant wind began to push the Armada northward. For two days, the English fleet followed; then, his own men dying in droves with scurvy and fever, Howard returned to port.

La Invencible Armada would never return to trouble the waters of the Channel. Only sixty of the Catholic horde survived the expedition — the wreckage of the remainder still rests along the shores of Scotland and Ireland. In England, Elizabeth and her people gave thanks to their Protestant God for his mercy, and praised the many brave men who had defeated the Spanish abomination. But in Spain, and throughout Catholic Europe, one man's name remained tied to the defeat of the Armada — *El Draque*. That Protestant devil had breathed his flames upon the harbor of Calais, and Philip's Great Endeavor had crumbled before it. However, as those who had looked in vain for Drake's lantern knew, it was perhaps too much credit for a man who had fought for his God and fought for his queen — until he saw the opportunity for plunder.

Chapter 5

The Final Raids

Even as the first English ships returned to port, military logic dictated that a strike be attempted on the Spanish coast. The Armada would take weeks to fetch home port, and during that time the coastal towns and shipping of the Iberian Peninsula would be vulnerable. It was even possible that the scattered vessels of the Great Endeavor could be destroyed piecemeal, broken and diseased as they would be by the time they arrived in home waters.

Unfortunately for Elizabeth, reality trumped logic. Her ships, foul within and without, needed repairs after months at sea. Scurvy and fevers riddled the ranks of the brave men who had thwarted the will of Philip II. Where few had fallen to the Spaniards, hundreds now died each day. Worse, from Elizabeth's perspective, the monies required to field England's defensive forces had drained the royal treasury by an alarming degree. England needed a respite, however brief, to restore ships, crews, and economy to health.

Sir Francis Drake, despite the opinions of some of his peers, still enjoyed the status of royal favorite — he was the only captain to recover substantial plunder, from the *Rosario,* at least a portion of which had made its way into Elizabeth's treasury—but missed the opening stages of planning the next move against Spain. He had fallen victim to one of the fevers raging through the fleet. Upon his recovery, Drake, in concert with an old acquaintance from his time in Ireland, Sir John Norris, immediately pushed for a new expedition. They planned to capture Lisbon, placing Dom Antonio on the throne of Portugal in the process. To Drake, an indebted Portugal offered much to England—secure bases for continued action against Spain and ready markets for English goods. Elizabeth, however, had reservations about Dom Antonio, and certainly had plans of her own.

First, Dom Antonio lacked money. Any outlay for the expedition would be a further drain on Elizabeth's dwindling fiscal reserves with no immediate return on the investment. Second, Dom Antonio was a Catholic, which did not promise long term support from Portugal for Protestant England. Finally, Elizabeth did not think that the peasantry of Portugal would risk life and limb simply to replace one master with another—the effort stood little chance of success. Rather than chase the chimera of a free and allied Portugal, Elizabeth desired concrete results with a quick return on her investment. She wanted a repetition of Drake's raid on Cádiz, the destruction of Spanish warships in their harbors and the capture of treasure ships (preferably the entire treasure fleet from the Americas).

As the project matured, costs remained a tremendous concern for Elizabeth. She dispatched Norris to the Netherlands, hoping to secure Dutch support for the expedition. Norris returned with the good news that both men and warships would be forthcoming, but amid diplomatic confusion, somehow the promised forces never materialized. Likewise, Dom Antonio had received a commitment from the ruler of Morocco to provide support in exchange for aid against the Spanish. This, too, never occurred. The pretender, at the insistence of Drake and Norris, also promised to repay most of the costs of the expedition as soon as he gained the throne. The problem with that promise is rather obvious.[1] In the end, the entire project became a joint public and private venture (as had been the raid on Cádiz), though the queen bore the brunt of the costs. With that in mind, she dictated the objectives to Drake, who would serve as Lord Admiral of the force.

Those objectives were clear and practical. First, destroy the Spanish warships, including the survivors of the Armada, scattered in ports from the Bay of Biscay to Lisbon. Next, capture the treasure fleet from the West Indies. Finally, and only after the first two objectives had been met, attempt to place Dom Antonio on the throne of Portugal. To accomplish this, Drake commanded a fleet of some one hundred vessels and upwards of twenty thousand men, organized into five squadrons, each under a vice-admiral. His war council would include his squadron commanders and the captain-general of the thousands of soldiers in the fleet. It was, in essence, a counter-Armada, and the largest force that Drake had ever commanded. Why did Elizabeth, who had chosen Howard over Drake as commander of her defensive forces the previous year, now trust Sir Francis with a comparable responsibility?

The answer is simple. Drake had a knack for destruction, a nose for plunder, and the luck that invariably accompanies perseverance and experience. None of her sea dogs had returned a tenth of the profits gleaned by Sir Francis, and no other captain caused Spaniards to quake in fear at the mere mention of his name. If any man could accomplish her desires, then it was this man who had dedicated his youth to learning piracy, and his adulthood to enriching his queen. If any man could destroy Philip's remaining warships and make Elizabeth rich in the process, it would be her Drake, her dragon, her raider extraordinare.

A queen's expectations may know no bounds, but those who must accomplish her will are mere mortals with very mortal limitations. Sir Francis Drake, leading this massive fleet from Plymouth on April 18, 1589, may not have realized his limitations. At age forty-nine, he had already exceeded the average life expectancy of his era. Still, the years had not been overly unkind.

Outwardly, Drake showed some widening of the girth, thinning of his reddish hair (now streaked with gray), and reduction of the strength and stamina that had amazed others in his youth. He had always experienced good health, and the bout with fever in the previous year suggests that age had reduced his natural resistance to disease—not a good sign for a commander who would repeatedly be exposed to stress, poor food, and numerous contagions while at sea.

More important, Drake had changed inwardly as well as outwardly. Gazing from the deck of his favorite flagship, the *Revenge,* he observed a fleet that stretched from horizon to horizon, and every pair of eyes seemed to turn to him for guidance. It was a far cry from the Cádiz raid of two years past. There he had only contended with one vice-admiral, and perhaps Drake realized that he should have handled Borough with more political astuteness. Now he had a council of six subcommanders, some of them favorites of the queen. Against the Armada, he had abandoned his squadron to plunder a ship. Drake could not have enjoyed the whispers of cowardice and treason from some of his fellow captains. Now he had to do far more than show a lantern at his stern for others to follow; he had to plan on a massive scale, then trust others to implement those plans. The past two years had given Sir Francis much to consider—perhaps too much.

No matter his state of mind and body, Drake began the endeavor in his typical piratical manner. To relieve the overcrowding on his vessels, he impressed a Dutch fleet of some sixty ships—after all, they were England's allies and, according to Norris, had promised to aid the expedition. Then he ignored a missive from the queen. She had discovered that her darling of the moment, the handsome Earl of Essex, had tired of playing pampered pet and stowed away on one of Drake's ships without her permission. Elizabeth demanded the immediate return of Essex, preferably with whoever had abetted him along in chains. Leaving Walsingham to smooth the royal feathers, Drake sailed onward.

Acting upon intelligence that as many as two hundred ships crowded the Spanish harbor of Corunna, Sir Francis arrived there on 24 April. Norris's soldiers quickly moved against the town, capturing sections of the city that had overflowed the protective fortifications of its original expanse. There they engaged in the usual looting and arson as well as the murder of numerous Catholic prisoners from the garrison. Meanwhile, Drake led his fleet against the harbor. In the old style, he personally commanded an assault on the island fortification guarding its entrance. But this time, Drake suffered a firm repulse. Worse, the harbor held fewer than a dozen ships, and the Spanish sailors burned the only valuable prize, a flagship from the Armada, rather than allow its capture. For the next two weeks, the expedition besieged the upper city of Corunna, Norris winning one pitched battle against a relief force during that time. In the end, the English effort was in vain. Drake lacked siege artillery to breach the walls, and the garrison of Corunna, having already observed the butchery of prisoners by the Protestant devils, fought an inspired battle.

As his men abandoned their siege, Drake faced an important decision. He could sail for the ports along the Bay of Biscay, looking into each and attempting to destroy any warships therein, but he had heard a rumor that a treasure ship had reached Peniche, a small coastal town some fifty miles from Lisbon. An assault there seemed a more profitable endeavor than burning warships. With Peniche taken, Norris would march overland to Lisbon, while Drake captured the port of Cascai, at the mouth of the Tagus River. Then, a secure base at his rear, Sir Francis would lead the fleet upriver for a joint attack on the city. If Lisbon could be taken in this pincer movement, a grateful Dom Antonio, once installed on the throne, would open the local treasury to pay for the expedition.

A decision could not wait; already, fever, compounded by an excess of local wine and the harsh Iberian sun, had made inroads into his command. Supported by his council, Drake opted to attack Lisbon—and ignored his queen's command to destroy the remnants of the Armada. Drake knew that success at Lisbon, especially sweetened with a treasure ship, would ease any anger at his disobedience.

On 16 May, Drake landed his army at the Portuguese port of Peniche. Norris, ably seconded by young Essex, drove the 5,000-strong Spanish garrison from the port in three days of heavy fighting. The English gained little from their efforts except dead and wounded men. The rumored treasure ship either never existed or had sailed away, and the town produced little in the way of plunder. Worse, Norris's regiments had expended a large quantity of their irreplaceable powder and shot. Nonetheless, Drake and his council decided to proceed with the attack on Lisbon, leaving several ships and a small garrison at Peniche. It took five days for the weakened forces under Norris, accompanied by a hopeful Dom Antonio, to march the fifty miles to Lisbon. Not surprisingly, the Spanish garrison knew that the English forces planned to attack and had prepared the city's defenses. The invaders, lacking artillery, could not breach Lisbon's thick walls without the help of the fleet. Short of munitions and faced with the fact that the Portuguese would not rally to the support of Dom Antonio, Norris could do little but anxiously await the arrival of Drake. The wait was in vain, and Norris abandoned the feeble siege, as well as his sick and wounded, on 26 May. The following day, the remnants of his force reached Cascai, to find Drake in the anchorage that he had controlled for the past six days.

Drake had seized the tiny port with ease on 20 May. It is uncertain what Drake did while his ships plundered the sparse local shipping, but he never attempted to capture or bypass the forts guarding the mouth of the Tagus. Did his nerve fail at the thought of ascending a narrow ten-mile stretch of river without local pilots? Was he sick with the fever that ravaged the fleet? Did he underestimate the time it would take for the soldiers to march to Lisbon? Drake's only statement on the matter is that he had planned to ascend the river on 27 May, an endeavor made pointless by Norris's return.

As the exhausted soldiers rested in Cascai, Drake's council voted to sail for the Azores. It appeared to be the most favorable place to intercept the treasure fleet and perhaps to gather support for Dom Antonio. As the fleet embarked its battered regiments, Drake enjoyed a stroke of luck. An unwary gaggle of fifty or more Spanish ships loaded with naval stores entered the bay. This windfall allowed Drake to dismiss at last the unhappy Dutch ships impressed at Plymouth (several had already registered their displeasure by deserting). On 8 June, with a favorable wind blowing, the expedition prepared to raise anchors for the Azores, only to be confronted by a vessel dispatched by the queen. She demanded the return of Essex, or she would withdraw her support from the expedition. Faced with that ultimatum, Drake reluctantly sent ships to withdraw his men from the garrison at Peniche before returning with Essex, but they had already been massacred by vengeful Spaniards. Then he prepared to sail north along the Spanish coast on 9 June. Unfortunately, that morning found the fleet becalmed and beset by a squadron of Spanish galleys from Lisbon. Before the wind finally arose, the fleet lost six ships.

As rumors of the queen's distress, the fate of the Peniche garrison, and the loss of vessels to the galleys spread throughout the fleet, morale began to collapse. When Drake ordered an attack on Vigo, many captains simply kept their headings for home. Only two thousand men remained healthy enough for the successful assault against the undefended city. With its flames brightening the horizon, Drake decided to take the twenty best ships and healthiest men to search for the Spanish treasure fleet. He left Norris to lead the remainder to Plymouth. However, within hours of leaving the Iberian coast, Drake's reduced force felt the fury of an Atlantic storm. The younger Francis had laughed at such storms, but this older pirate seemed to lack the indomitable will of his youth. He bowed his head, and turned for England. Arriving in Plymouth in early July, Norris found a dejected Drake awaiting him.

At last, the famous luck of Sir Francis Drake had reached balance. The expedition's failure had been several orders of magnitude greater than Elizabeth would tolerate. Thousands of men had died of wounds or disease. Hundreds of the sick and injured had been abandoned and butchered by vengeful Spaniards. The survivors had often looted their own ships once reaching a safe haven, denying Elizabeth even a small measure of return on her investment. Drake had angered the Dutch, failed in his attempt to free Portugal, and single-handedly reversed the rapidly growing myth of Protestant invincibility. Worse, he had ignored her orders to destroy the remnants of the Armada, had failed to capture a single treasure ship, and had endangered her Earl of Essex.

Perhaps some measure of good luck did remain; at least Sir Francis retained his title and his personal wealth — as well as his head. However, Elizabeth no longer sought his advice or welcomed him at court. Some men would have remained in London, hoping for a reprieve from the queen. Others would have retired to their country homes to live their remaining years in peace. Sir Francis did neither; instead he remained active in the local life at Plymouth. Fearing a Spanish invasion, the town sought his help in putting the local defenses in order. Then, as the war with Spain continued, the queen's council named Drake as a prize commissioner for Plymouth. It was an interesting choice, placing an aging but unreformed pirate in charge of providing an inventory of prize goods.

As the years passed, Drake slowly regained the good graces of the queen. His longevity contributed to his restoration, as one by one the old sea dogs and favored advisers passed from the scene. Walsingham, the chancellor who had supported Drake more than once, died in 1590. The following year, Sir Francis probably gnashed his teeth when he heard that Sir Richard Grenville had lost his old flagship, the *Revenge,* to a horde of Spanish ships. Yet the way Grenville had died — from mortal wounds received after resisting impossible odds for a dozen hours — possibly appealed to Sir Francis. In fact, it may have encouraged him to seek one more raid, one final chance to recover former glory and to redeem his name. For help, he turned to the man with whom he had begun his career so many years ago, Sir John Hawkins.

Elizabeth tentatively approved an expedition under the joint leadership of Drake and Hawkins in late 1593, but the usual dithering over objectives and funding delayed even gathering the fleet until late the following year. Drake's experiences and wishes are obvious in the planning of 1594. Panama, storehouse of Spain's Pacific silver, must be the ultimate target of a land attack across the isthmus. By 1595, the queen sought a more limited objective — capture the treasure fleet from the West Indies as it passed through the Azores, watch for a Spanish invasion of Ireland, and return within six months. Both captains argued for the original objective, especially when rumor reached them that a severely damaged treasure ship had taken refuge at San Juan on the island of Puerto Rico. Elizabeth relented, though she now expected them to take that ship on the way to Panama.[2]

Drake's *Defiance* and Hawkins' *Garland* led two squadrons, totaling twenty-seven ships, from Plymouth on 28 August 1595. It is interesting to note that along with the knocked-down pinnaces and myriad supplies crowding his holds, Drake had decided to take his will with him. Within days, the two aging sea dogs fell to arguing when Drake, his holds filled with pinnaces instead of provisions, asked Hawkins to shift some of Drake's men to his ships. The older man refused. Then Sir Francis argued for an assault (in search of additional supplies) on Las Palmas in the Canaries. When Hawkins demurred, Drake threatened to attack with only his squadron, forcing his co-commander to relent.

The attack, complicated by high surf and alerted defenders, rapidly became a disaster. Worse, prisoners taken by the Spaniards revealed the entire plan. Soon fast couriers made for Spain, where Philip dispatched a fleet in search of the English, and for the West Indies. The raiding force had surrendered the tactical initiative to Spain. Drake and Hawkins, the older man now sick, should have realized this when they lost a ship (ironically named the *Francis*) to an alerted Indies Fleet shortly after reaching the island of Guadelupe. For almost two weeks, the raiders paused at that island, assembling pinnaces and mounting the cannon that had been stored in holds during the Atlantic crossing. Perhaps

Drake also hoped that a short rest would allow Hawkins to recover.

That hope was in vain, for Hawkins, the somewhat reformed pirate who had contributed much to building Elizabeth's navy, died on 11 May, shortly after the fleet anchored at Puerto Rico. Two days later, Sir Francis personally led a night assault on the harbor at San Juan. Stiff resistance resulted in heavy losses for both sides but only one Spanish vessel burned by Drake and his men. That same day, a disappointed Drake abandoned the venture, briefly rested his men and repaired his vessels at an isolated bay, then sailed for the Spanish Main.

The end of November found Drake in the familiar waters of the Main. He seized the town of Río de la Hacha, stripped and abandoned by its forewarned inhabitants. Following the old pattern, he attempted to extort ransom from the local authorities, who proved more than happy to negotiate, but less than willing to pay. At last realizing that a Spanish fleet probably pursued him, Drake torched much of the town and sailed away. On 20 November, Sir Francis raided the village of Santa Marta, gaining little in plunder. Leaving columns of smoke to mark his passing, he then sailed for Nombre de Dios and an overland expedition against Panama.

That tiny port had changed little since Drake's last visit many years earlier. Seizing it on 27 December, Drake immediately disembarked his soldiers, and some eight hundred or so began the trek to Panama. The soldiers discovered that the poverty of Nombre de Dios seemed to be the only thing on the isthmus that had remained the same. Spanish soldiers had removed the threat of the local *negros cimarrones,* the only potential allies for the English. Even the old mule trail had shifted north, forcing the raiders to hack a path for themselves. Worse, Spanish soldiers barred that path from an improvised fort. They easily thwarted assaults by the lightly armed raiders. Without hope of success, the survivors returned to Nombre de Dios. A despondent Drake embarked his troops and burned the town on 5 January 1596.

By that date, sickness ravaged the fleet. For only the second time on record, Drake succumbed to one of his sailors' illnesses. His "bloody flux," diarrhea and fever, worsened over the next weeks, as contrary winds forced the fleet away from the Main and into the Caribbean. Soon, Drake could no longer walk the deck of his own ship. He ordered the fleet to stop at a small island for some days of rest and repair; then, on 24 January, Drake set sails for Puerto Bello, unwilling to return to England without some plunder in his holds. Within three days, Drake raved with fever. In a final moment of clarity, he completed his will and donned his armor to await the final judgment of his God. Sometime in the early morning of 28 January 1596, Drake passed away. His men placed him in a lead-lined coffin, and buried him at sea. Even as his mortal remains descended into the murky depths, the old pirate who had feared his God, sometimes obeyed his queen, and died while reaching for a final bit of plunder, ascended into the realm of English myth.

Chapter 6

Who Was Francis Drake?

CICERO, ONE OF the greatest minds of ancient Rome, once claimed that history, as one of the liberal arts, should only be taught by orators and poets. Anyone who has endured the seemingly endless hours of deadly droning from yellowed notes when the modern tenure process confuses scholarship with teaching ability can understand the need for skilled orators. Comprehending Cicero's request for poets as teachers is a little more difficult. Yet take this verse, penned by the poet Greepe in 1587, to mark the achievements of an English sailor:

> Ulysses with his navy great
> In ten years' time great valour won;
> Yet all his time did no such feat
> As Drake within one year hath done.
> Both Turk and Pope and all our foes
> Do dread this Drake wher'er he goes.[1]

Greepe, in six short and easily memorized lines, filled the hearts of Englishmen with pride in a national achievement, catapulted Drake into the ranks of mythical captains, and established an ideal of naval valor for generations of seafarers to emulate. Poets such as Greepe touch the heart's strings, arousing the emotions at our core and teaching us what it means to be human. At the same time, they give us pride in our nationality, be that American, British, Chinese, or even Roman. For Cicero, orators could eloquently explain the world around us, but poets, tapping our innermost experiences, could best define exactly who we were within that world. Who, then, was Francis Drake, and what experiences shaped his path to legendary status?

The early years are the most formative in any life. Drake's common birth, as the lack of records attests, did not bode well for his chances at achieving immortality — only dust marks the passage of most such lives. Once the family became religious refugees reduced to living in rented space aboard a ruined hulk, the odds grew even longer that Drake's name would ever be entered into the pages of history. But his parents certainly provided the lad with guidance and some small opportunity to better himself. As the eldest of a large brood of children in an apparently closely knit family, Francis quickly developed elementary leadership skills. Later, one or more of his siblings would join him on every expedition. There the older brother would continue to teach them, attempt to shield them from harm, and mourn their passing when his efforts failed.

The place of religion — and religious persecution — in Drake's youth must be stressed. At his father's feet, he learned to hate Catholicism as well as the English Catholics who forced the Drakes from their family home and into destitute circumstances. He also learned from his parents to love a Protestant God. And, as Protestant doctrine stressed the individual's comprehension of the Bible, Edmund Drake gave his son a gift denied most commoners in Europe: the ability to read and write. Though the boy would never become a scholar, literacy was a necessary tool to enter into the world of seafaring merchants. Also, it would have been a prerequisite for the fostering of the young man into another Protestant household.

The time spent as a fosterling with the Hawkins family seems critical to the development of the future sea dog. As Drake learned to be a seaman and a merchant, he absorbed the social skills of a new class of wealthy Englishmen—a rising mercantile bourgeoisie that itself aped the styles of the old noble families. Drake, however, would always carry some of the mannerisms and voice patterns of his youth—damning in the class-conscious upper strata of English society. The years with the Hawkins family undoubtedly shaped the expectations of their poorer cousin. His driving desire to join the privileged elite (which he had only viewed from the outside), as well as the need to be loved and accepted by others (even if bought with gifts), may well have formed during those years.

From his extended family, Drake also learned the path that he would later exploit to reach his personal goals—piracy. English merchants had little choice except to play the part-time corsair. Spain and Portugal had closed most of the world's markets to them while France and an emergent Netherlands competed fiercely with England for the remaining trade. As long as the English monarch winked at purloined goods and vessels, the game continued. Elizabeth, of course, knew how to wink.

The relationship of Elizabeth I to her sea dogs also shaped Drake. In the great game of nations played by England's queen, even her favored captains remained pawns. They knew that to be the case, and were very alert to the concept of sacrificing a pawn in pursuit of eventual victory. Thus, Drake and others of his ilk tended to enter home ports with care when returning from plundering abroad—whether executions were done from national necessity or royal whimsy, hanged remained hanged. On the other hand, brilliant success always roused Elizabeth's smile and could result in the pawn's advancement to the highest possible rank—knight. Yet, once there, the sea dogs discovered that knights could be sacrificed almost as readily as pawns.

In some sense, Drake's own leadership style reflected that of his queen. The men who sailed with him were pawns, and he sacrificed them in pursuit of victory just as readily as his queen would have offered up Drake if necessary. Like his queen, the captain rewarded success, though he always retained as much of the plunder as possible for himself (again, no difference there). Drake also seemed to emulate Elizabeth in one other important way. He tolerated no disloyalty within his shipboard realm, and readily dispensed death for any suspected treason as well as lesser transgressions. Unfortunately, Drake's own loyalty to anyone but himself sometimes appeared in doubt. When his luck finally failed, it was the fact that he had (more than once) disobeyed direct orders, rather than the failure itself, that cost Sir Francis his queen's favor.

Was Drake simply lucky? Or was he an extremely talented naval commander? *Fortuna* seems to grin at those who work hardest for success, and Drake certainly applied a tremendous amount of effort to his piracy. As a tactical leader, his personal strength, courage, and persistence in the face of adversity remain admirable. Drake's observation and analysis during his early voyages led to brilliant successes when he later commanded his first expeditions to the New World. He was an acknowledged master of the daring strike against unprepared enemies and the sudden raid with limited forces.

Yet a disturbing pattern emerged in Drake's later years—he became a creature of habit. His assaults on ports, no matter the size of forces involved, remained night attacks by land coupled with a direct naval assault on the harbor. If successful (at least in the Caribbean), he followed the old pattern of ransom, regardless of both fiscal realities and the larger number of troops involved. In his last expedition, Drake loaded his holds with knocked-down pinnaces instead of food despite the greater number of mouths to feed, forcing the fleet into abortive attacks simply to reprovision before ever reaching its objectives in the West Indies. Worse, his fleets followed the same routes—as if he expected the Spaniards to remain unresponsive to the painful learning of lessons past.

Yes, Drake was lucky—and Drake was a fine naval commander, until age robbed him of the vision of his youth. If he served himself first from the plunder of Spain, a charge of which he often stood accused, then certainly he served his Protestant God and his mercurial queen just as gladly when England's enemies pressed upon that isle. And, in truth, his spirit serves them still.

In Buckland Abbey, there waits a very special drum — Drake's Drum. Like Drake himself, that drum remains a part of English folklore. The legend goes that when England is in a time of direst need, when the hated Spaniard again ascends the Channel, beating that drum will cause Drake to appear and once again serve the land of his birth. But the spirit Drake embodied has never really gone away.

That spirit could have been seen on Nelson's deck at Trafalgar, or at Beatty's shoulder at Jutland, or in the young flyer who risked his life to slam the fatal torpedo into Germany's *Bismarck,* or in the British marines who stormed ashore in the Falklands.

In every crisis, at every hard turn, wherever his country has struggled, Drake's essence was there. For he is more than the man who feared his God, served his queen, and loved his plunder — Sir Francis Drake is part and parcel of the indomitable spirit of the English people.

Notes

Chapter 2

1. Harry Kelsey, *Sir Francis Drake: The Queen's Pirate* (New Haven, CT: Yale University Press, 1998), 3–7; Ernle Bradford, *The Wind Commands Me: A Life of Sir Francis Drake* (New York: Harcourt, Brace and World, 1965), 28.
2. Kelsey, *Sir Francis Drake,* 409–411.
3. Reprinted in Derek Wilson, *The World Encompassed: Francis Drake and His Great Voyage* (New York: Harper & Row, 1977).
4. Bradford, *The Wind Commands Me,* 30–31.
5. Kelsey, *Sir Francis Drake,* 9–10.
6. John Hampden, ed., *Francis Drake, Privateer* (Tuscaloosa: University of Alabama Press, 1972), 37.

Chapter 3

1. Kelsey, *Sir Francis Drake,* 48.
2. *Pasha* has been rendered as *Pasco* and *Pascoe* by various scholars, sometimes with a capacity of as little as 40 tons, a debatable figure considering crew size and items stored within its hold.
3. Hampden, *Francis Drake, Privateer,* 128. Estimates of the *Pelican's* tonnage range from 100 to 150. The tonnage used is that quoted in *The World Encompassed,* first printed in 1628.
4. Derek Wilson, *The World Encompassed: Francis Drake and His Great Voyage* (New York: Harper and Row, 1977), 151–165.
5. Ibid., 190.

Chapter 4

1. Kelsey, *Sir Francis Drake,* 255–256.
2. Note that this was the predecessor of the famous Lost Colony of Roanoke, which would be settled in July 1587.

3. As quoted in Bradford, *The Wind Commands Me,* 169.
4. "Sir Francis Drake to Walsyngham, April 2, 1587," in Julian S. Corbett, ed., *Papers Relating to the Navy during the Spanish War, 1585–1587* (London: Navy Records Society, 1898), 102–104.
5. "Drake to Walsyngham, May 17, 1587," Corbett, *Papers,* 131–134.
6. Colin Martin and Geoffrey Parker, *The Spanish Armada* (New York: W. W. Norton, 1988), 34–35.
7. Ibid., 36–37.

Chapter 5
1. Kelsey, *Sir Francis Drake,* 346–347.
2. Ibid., 378–379.

Chapter 6
1. As quoted in Wade G. Dudley, "Drake at Cadiz," in Samuel A. Southworth, ed., *Great Raids in History: From Drake to Desert One* (New York: Sarpedon, 1997), 20.

Selected Bibliography

Andrews, Kenneth R., ed. *The Last Voyage of Drake and Hawkins.* Cambridge, UK: Hakluyt Society, 1972.

Bradford, Ernle. *The Wind Commands Me: A Life of Sir Francis Drake.* New York: Harcourt, Brace and World, 1965.

Corbett, Julian S. *Drake and the Tudor Navy with a History of the Rise of England as a Maritime Power.* 2 vols. New York: Burt Franklin, 1899.

Corbett, Julian S., ed. *Papers Relating to the Navy during the Spanish War, 1585–1587.* London: Navy Records Society, 1898.

Drake, Sir Francis. *The World Encompassed.* Introduction by W. S. W. Vaux. London: Hakluyt Society, 1854.

Dudley, Wade G. "Drake at Cadiz" in Samuel A. Southworth, ed. *Great Raids in History: From Drake to Desert One.* New York: Sarpedon, 1997, pp. 7-20.

Guy, John. *Tudor England.* New York: Oxford University Press, 1990.

Hampden, John, ed. *Francis Drake, Privateer: Contemporary Narratives and Documents.* Tuscaloosa: University of Alabama Press, 1972.

Harland, John. *Seamanship in the Age of Sail.* Annapolis, MD: Naval Institute Press, 1996.

Kelsey, Harry. *Sir Francis Drake: The Queen's Pirate.* New Haven, CT: Yale University Press, 1998.

László, Veres, and Richard Woodman. *The Story of Sail.* Annapolis, MD: Naval Institute Press, 1999.

Martin, Colin, and Geoffrey Parker. *The Spanish Armada.* New York: W. W. Norton, 1988.

Mattingly, Garrett. *The Armada.* Boston: Houghton Mifflin, 1959.

Palliser, D. M. *The Age of Elizabeth: England under the Late Tudors, 1547–1603.* New York: Longman, 1983.

Thrower, Norman J. W., ed. *Sir Francis Drake and the Famous Voyage, 1577–1580.* Berkeley, CA: University of California Press, 1984.

Wagner, Henry R. *Sir Francis Drake's Voyage Around the World: Its Aims and Achievements.* San Francisco: John Howell Books, 1926.

Williams, Penry. *The Tudor Regime.* New York: Oxford University Press, 1981.

Wilson, Derek. *The World Encompassed: Francis Drake and His Great Voyage.* New York: Harper and Row, 1977.

Index

About the Author

Wade G. Dudley is a visiting assistant professor at East Carolina University in Greenville, North Carolina. He holds a master's degree in maritime history and nautical archaeology from East Carolina University and a doctorate in history from the University of Alabama at Tuscaloosa. Professor Dudley is a specialist in early European military and naval history. He lives in Winterville, North Carolina.